THE
ENDGAME OF
GLOBALIZATION

THE
ENDGAME OF
GLOBALIZATION

NEIL SMITH

Routledge
New York • London

Published in 2005 by
Routledge
270 Madison Avenue
New York, NY 10016
www.routledge-ny.com

Published in Great Britain by
Routledge
2 Park Square
Milton Park, Abingdon,
Oxon OX14 4RN
www.routledge.co.uk

Routledge is an imprint of the Taylor & Francis Group.
Printed in the United States of America on acid-free paper.

Smith, Neil.
  The endgame of globalization / Neil Smith.
    p. cm.
  Includes bibliographical references and index.
  ISBN 0-415-95012-0 (hb : alk. paper)
  1. United States--Foreign relations--1989- 2. Geopolitics--United
States. 3. Globalization--History. 4. Liberalism--United States. I.
Title.

  E895.S63 2005
  327.73'009'0511--dc22   2004023476

TABLE OF CONTENTS

PREFACE   vii

1.   ENDGAME GEOGRAPHIES   1

2.   LIBERALISM AND THE ROOTS OF AMERICAN
     GLOBALISM   28

3.   A GLOBAL MONROE DOCTRINE?   53

4.   "A HALF LOAF": BRETTON WOODS, THE UN, AND
     THE SECOND MOMENT OF US AMBITION   82

5.   THE WHOLE LOAF?: GLOBALIZATION   122

6.   GUANTÁNAMO CONVENTIONS: THE BANKRUPTCY
     OF LIBERALISM   149

7.   THE ENDGAME OF GLOBALIZATION: AFTER IRAQ   177

ENDNOTES   211

INDEX   219

PREFACE

The transition from 1990s neoliberalism to twenty-first century neoconservatism in the United States, punctuated by the aftermath of September 11, 2001, has come to be understood across the political spectrum as one of the sharpest political swings in recent US history. This book argues, on the contrary, that while these Democratic and Republican administrations were led by quite opposite personalities, voiced very different rhetorics, and were fired by radically divergent intellectual traditions—not to mention the different sectors of the American polity they appealed to—over a longer term and in international perspective, the continuity since the 1980s era, which first announced globalization, far outreaches the discontinuities. War in Afghanistan and especially in Iraq is widely seen as a decisive break with the Washington Consensus that came to prevail in the 1990s, and quite reasonably so. Far from a consensus, war has rapidly isolated the United States in a world that better understands or admits how much of a failure that war quickly became. But it is necessary to take a broader view.

For better or worse, the Iraq war does not represent such a radical break with prior US global ambition. A good claim can be made, in fact, that this war represents the endgame of globalization. It is not a "war on terrorism" so much as a war to finish off a larger and longer term project. War in Iraq should be comprehended as part of a US globalism that, on the one hand, is rooted in the eighteenth-century liberalism out of which the US emerged and, on the other, began to gain full expression in the early twentieth century. However much it goes against our inherited twentieth century sense of political order concerning the difference between liberals and conservatives, George W. Bush has to be seen historically—as much as (if not more than) the Democrats who oppose him—as the heir of Woodrow Wilson and Franklin Roosevelt. What makes the present moment so dangerous is that while neither of these earlier presidents started the wars that became vehicles to their global ambitions, this time it was an American president who started the Iraq war, and extrication is therefore unlikely to be a simple matter.

The book proceeds quite straightforwardly. In chapter one, I contrast the origins of Iraq in 1920 with its contentious loss of sovereignty more than eight decades later, using this to highlight specific contradictions of US globalism. The following chapter examines the historical and philosophical background, locating American globalism and empire in their liberal roots. In chapters three and four I examine the rise and fall of US global power in two prior moments of global ambition: respectively, the years leading up to and surrounding the first and second world wars. Wilson, with his global Monroe Doctrine, and Roosevelt, with his new world order, are the central figures in these episodes. Chapter five considers the rise of so-called globalization, following the economic crises and restructurings of the 1970s and the implosion of the only other political superpower, and it traces the reemergence of US global designs toward century's end. The penultimate chapter gathers together the discussions of liberalism and the history of US global aspirations to discuss the symptomatic bankruptcy of liberalism under the new "Guantánamo conventions" which guide US international behavior in the post-9/11 world. It argues that this does not constitute a "war on terrorism," but rather a continuation of globalization by military means. Finally, chapter seven reconsiders the contradictions of US liberalism in the light of war and argues that far from a triumphal endgame to globalization, as its architects—Republicans *and* Democrats—intended, this third moment of US imperial assertion is also slouching toward defeat.

No book is an individual effort and I have benefited from a lot of assistance even though—perhaps because—the manuscript was finished quickly. Megan Schauer at the Center for Place, Culture, and Politics at the CUNY Graduate Center deserves special thanks not only for ordering my chaotic workplace in such a way that I could take time to write, but for considerable assistance tracking down, with speed and efficiency, both tiny details and big ideas for this book.

Mike Lamb and Laura Kaehler were also indispensable at the Center. Indeed, the many fellows who have now passed through the Center have provided the most stimulating environment in which to work out some of these ideas. I especially want to thank Omar Dahbour, Associate Director of the Center, who never lets me get away with fuzzy thinking, and Christian Parenti, whose intrepid journalism is inspiring. Many other friends and colleagues at the Grad Center have also been supportive: Julian Brash, Eliza Darling, Tina Harris, David Harvey, Cindi Katz, Bill Kelly, Anders Lund Hansen, Ida Susser, and too many more to enumerate. And where would I be without the dedicated service of those at my second office—John and Jackie, Owen and Dolores.

Given the nature of the book, I also owe a great debt to many journalists around the world who, often at considerable risk to both body and career, have slashed through the veil of not so subtle censorship, intensified so dramatically in recent years, to give us all a glimpse, if we make the effort to look, of how the endgame of globalization actually unfolds. Susan Fainstein introduced me to Louis Hartz, whose work helped me crystallize ideas and connections that I only vaguely grasped before. Then there is my editor Dave McBride who, I have to say, has been generous and insightful and fully involved with the book—better than any writer could ever expect—and who in the process became a friend.

Finally, as deadlines got tight, Deb Cowen read the entire manuscript and laced her comments and suggestions with her usual sharp yet sensitive intelligence. She is supportive in a million other ways, and I look forward to reciprocating such a beautiful gift.

1

ENDGAME GEOGRAPHIES

"World domination, the same old story. The world is full of
people who think they are Napoleon or God."

Sean Connery as James Bond, *Dr. No*, 1962

Baghdad, April 9, 2003. With the cameras of the global media ex-
citedly in place, the toppling of the statue of Saddam Hussein begins. Several dozen jubilant Iraqi men throng around the base
while a US marine scales the statue and drapes Saddam's head
with a large Stars and Stripes. It remains there for a few minutes
while a jib and chain from a US half-track tank are attached to
Hussein's neck. Another climber replaces the red, white, and blue
with an Iraqi flag. The statue is soon pulled over, bending to the
plaza floor amid cheers all around. Beamed across the world, this
image quickly became iconic of the end of Iraq's dictatorship and
the imminent victory of the massive US-led invasion force.
Endgame Saddam.

If the orchestration of this photo-op by US marines was readily apparent, the contradictions it expressed may have been less so. Washington always forcefully insisted that this was a war and invasion carried out by an international coalition, not simply the United States, and yet for US marines in Baghdad their own national symbol was an appropriate—even natural—symbol of victory for global good. The nascent contradiction between narrow nationalist interests on the one hand and the claim to embody global right on the other was neither accidental nor arbitrary, but tapped deep and long-held aspirations for an American globalism. If the exuberance of the moment swept away all such public recognition, US marine colonels on the eve of war were much more astute. Anticipating the revelatory power of just such a scenario, they had quietly but firmly frowned on nationalist ostentation, ordering the flag kept under wraps. Its appearance on Saddam's head was in any event widely understood around the world as a more triumphalist kind of endgame, an increasingly accomplished US political and economic hegemony in the world: endgame global America.

The substitution of the Iraqi for the American flag on Saddam's head opened the prospect of an alternative, however. It was initially met with a certain patronizing jollity—"isn't that nice for the poor Iraqis who now have their country back"—but in retrospect, as war and invasion turned into quagmire and continuous civil strife, this scene may yet prove to have a more prophetic meaning. Rather than buttressing America's enthronement as political, economic, and military hegemon, opposition to the war and subsequent occupation of Iraq may well provoke a different result: "endgame lost."[1]

Iraq 1920/2005

Prior to 1920, Iraq did not exist. It was created that year as a British mandate after a bitter contest over the area's future, and ultimately became an independent nation-state in 1932. Three quarters of a century later, it lost that sovereignty after a US-led invasion, and today it sits as the epicenter around which future US global power will be arbitrated.

Consolidated in the wake of World War I from three provinces in the crumbling Ottoman Empire—Basra, Baghdad and Mosul—the new state was administered under League of Nations mandate. The British administration was predictably dismissive of local ambitions and demands, and in early 1920 opposition grew, especially among the southern Shi'a who had been suppressed by the Ottomans in favor of the northern Sunnis. The British were bent on repeating the Ottoman divide-and-conquer strategy, but they were challenged by a Shi'a-led coalition seeking Iraqi independence. After a series of demonstrations and violent revolts against British occupation, a full-scale armed uprising broke out in June 1920. The Kurds piled on, rising against a resurgent Turkish military that threatened a reprise of Ottoman control in Kurdish towns and terrain. The jerry-rigged nation-state, it was clear, would be difficult to manage, and the British military responded forcefully. Over several months, they suppressed the Iraqi revolt at the cost of an estimated 6,000 Iraqi lives and approximately 500 Indian and British troops.

The similarities with 2005 are significant except that the more recent invasion is American-led rather than British, is more deadly, and is more prolonged—but probably just as futile. More than 1,000 US troops have been killed in less than eighteen months, and the number of Iraqi fatalities quickly doubled the 1920 toll as civil strife spiraled out of control. An interim government has been widely recognized as a puppet for US power. Even with 135,000–150,000 troops on the ground, the US has been unable to pacify the country—indeed it was forced to retreat from several large cities—and faces a growing crisis. Like the British after 1920, the US wants control of Iraq at arm's length. Ideally, they would like to extract themselves, but like the British again they hardly know how to accomplish this as the mess of occupation magnifies.

The historical geography of the 1920 uprising is instructive. From bases in India, Britain had invaded the southern city of Basra in late 1914 after the Ottoman Empire joined Germany and the other "Central Powers" at the advent of World War I. Their "military expedition" sought to break almost four centuries of Ottoman power over the region—an Asian continuation of long-term European efforts against Muslim powers. After serious military setbacks, the British eventually took Baghdad in March 1917 and Mosul a year later. Meanwhile, the evanescent 1916 Sykes-Picot agreement between the colonial powers of Britain and France envisaged a division of the Ottoman Middle East: the French would take much of present-day Syria, while the British claimed prerogative over a possibly independent Palestine and control of the Transjordan, as it was then known, together with the three provinces that eventually became Iraq (including latter-day Kuwait). While giving lip-service to the possibility of independence, the British moved to control these new territories from Delhi as much as from London. The new regional borders were still amorphous, and the British refused to allow an official Iraqi delegation to be represented at the all-important Paris Peace Conference in 1919.

United under British rule, leaders in the three provinces cautiously forged closer political ties among the Shi'a of the south, the favored Sunnis based largely in and around Baghdad and the north, and the Kurds from Mosul and the Turkish borderlands in the northeast. Then as now, the majority Shi'a anticipated taking control and assumed the elite Sunni, who had enjoyed greater influence under the Ottoman state, would be sidelined. But that did not happen. Shi'a tribal leaders, who enjoyed longstanding local loyalty based on relations of land ownership, water rights, the authority to tax, and religious fealty, were themselves marginalized.

A March 1921 conference in Cairo was organized and controlled by that billy-goat-gruff of the British Empire, then colonial secretary Winston Churchill, and attended by numerous Arab officials from the region. It mandated that a separate territory of Iraq would become a kingdom and that Faisal, the Hashemite Amir, would be placed on the throne. Faisal had little immediate connection to the three provinces—his father had been the sharif of distant Mecca in present-day Saudi Arabia—but he was recommended due to his leadership of the so-called "Arab Revolt" that sided with the invading British in the war against the traditional Ottoman occupier. A significant if sometimes reluctant British ally, Faisal was more than a puppet but hardly more than "sovereign of a state that itself was not sovereign."[2]

Iraqis were broadly opposed to the British mandate, not just in the center but at the edges. In 1922 the Turkish military, vanquished in the war, moved back into the Kurdish area of Mosul.

There, the the British overseeing the territory let the Turks discipline the Kurds before responding with Royal Air Force
indignation. The British not only routed the Turks, but in 1924
forced the local Kurdish leader into Persian exile. Hopes for an
autonomous Kurdistan waned as the British and Turks effectively
split the Kurds between Turkey, Iraq, Iran, and Syria. Various
treaties throughout the 1920s established Iraq's geographical
boundaries vis-à-vis its six neighbors, producing the tell-tale
straight lines of imperial imposition on the region's map.

Their imperialism facing exhaustion, the British slowly realized in the 1920s that they could not control the new Iraq. The
old strategy of territorial control was bankrupt, but control at
arm's length was a different matter, and a series of assemblies and
parliaments beholden to London was organized. While they
pushed for Iraqi entry into the League of Nations—a stamp of
global legitimacy—the British also worked their economic interests. German and Ottoman shares in the Turkish Petroleum
Company, which had located large oil reserves, were already liqui-
dated, and the British grabbed and reorganized corporate ownership of Iraqi oil in favor of British capital (47.5 percent shared
equally between Royal Dutch Shell and the Anglo-Persian Oil
Company [later British Petroleum—BP]). The French, in com-
pensation for their acquiescence over Jordan and Palestine, received 23.75 percent and the Americans another 23.75 percent
(shared equally between Standard Oil of New Jersey and Mobil).
Despite a 1920 promise, the British thereby froze the Iraqis out of
any real control—5 percent was left—over their own oil, in lieu of
royalty payments. Oil was tapped in Kirkuk in 1927, and a
pipeline to the Mediterranean was completed eight years later.

With the oil agreement in place, a 1930 Anglo-Iraqi treaty announced the end of the British mandate and Iraqi independence.
While getting some of what they wanted, the British realized
the need to get out of an Iraq that they sensed would be impervious to external control. And they were eventually successful in retaining significant economic control of new, vast and growing oil
resources without the headaches of political and territorial control. There was of course much intervening history, but essentially the same dilemma faced the United States after 2003. Again,
many Iraqis have not been entirely antagonistic to a foreign-
sponsored intervention, this time aimed at overthrowing a widely
despised dictator. And again the crucial question becomes how to
amalgamate disparate political, geographical and religious
groups into some kind of national unity, or else how to organize
an alternative.

Much like the British in 1920, the United States today struggles
to establish territorial control and promote a favorable local
regime that will support US economic prerogatives. The Bush administration—at least its dominant Defense wing—evidently believed that the military overthrow of Hussein would be the hard
part and that flowers and kisses for invading troops would grease
the wheels of an effortless reconstruction of *comprador* power.
The comparisons with 1920 are again instructive. The US administration has been astonishingly naive in believing that the Iraqi
population would cede national control to an invading power
that breathes the flames of imperial ambition—a self-described
"crusade"—in the Middle East. As one historian wrote of the
British in 1920: "Once in, it was difficult to get out."[3]

'We Are All Americans Now'

The powering of commercial planes into the World Trade Center and the Pentagon in 2001 were highly local events yet at the same time utterly global. They certainly elicited a global response. Sympathy for the immediate victims—more than 2,700 New Yorkers hailing from some 90 countries, 180 military personnel and employees in Washington DC, and 40 people on a downed plane in Pennsylvania—came from everywhere as the gruesome results of the attacks played out in real time on television and computer screens around the world. From Seoul to Cairo, Moscow to Santiago, and throughout the Middle East, there were candlelight vigils and other sympathetic demonstrations deploring the attacks on New York and Washington. Horror mixed with widespread apprehension over the embarrassing ease of the attacks. That they seemed to come from nowhere raised the specter of a sudden escalation of terrorist threats from which no one was safe. Especially for those who had traveled to New York—less so the antiseptic space around the Pentagon—the depth of global empathy with the United States was extraordinary. German Chancellor Gerhard Schröder, reciprocating the cross-border Cold War comradery of John F. Kennedy four decades earlier ("Ich bin ein Berliner"), expressed the new sense of global vulnerability and affinity in the same terms: "we are all Americans now." "We are all Americans," insisted the September 12, 2001 banner headline in the French newspaper, *Le Monde*.

In some strange way we *were* all Americans after September 11, 2001. But how and why? Certainly not because September 11th was in any way the most deadly act of terrorism we have known or because it claimed an inordinate number of lives in the annals of human violence: after the ethnic cleansing of Bosnia and Kosovo in the early 1990s we were not all suddenly oppressed Muslims; after the Central African genocide of the mid-1990s— at the expense of perhaps 700,000 lives—the citizens of the world did not all become Tutsis; nor did we become Timorese nor Palestinians nor Guatemalan peasants. After the horrific bombing of trains in Madrid in 2004, we did not all become Spaniards, nor Russians after Beslan. A certain racism—perhaps more accurately a sense of some differential value of citizens from different groups, countries, or hemispheres—surely framed some of the differential response to September 11th, and the global power of US-owned and controlled media, for whose executives these events were obviously highly personal, accentuated the response. Certainly too the spectacular nature of the attacks—the targets, execution, symbolism, and instantaneous worldwide transmission of the falling towers—seared them into our global imagination. After all, the United States stood as the world's remaining superpower, apparently inviolate, assuredly powerful, yet suddenly and somehow an underdog in a fight few perceived it was even in. But this remains only a partial account. Just as powerful is the close connection that many people feel around the world to the expression of "America"—quite distinct from the US government—as a place where they might also experience a different kind of life, temporarily or permanently, in practice or vicariously. This ideology is as old as it is powerful in the modern world and it was very easily called up, both deliberately and spontaneously, by the events of 2001 and by responses to them. The wound of September 11th was also a wound to this psychic comfort afforded across national and cultural borders. It spoke to us all just as the Stars and Stripes over Saddam's head was meant to do nineteen months later.

To say this is not to succumb to right-wing and nationalist ideologies about American greatness—love it or leave it—nor does it confuse the power of the myth for the less salubrious reality of millions of people's daily lives inside and outside the United States. The mythology of America sits uncomfortably with the reality of 36 million people, disproportionately minorities, living in poverty within its own boundaries. But it does suggest the importance of such deep-seated global desires attached to this specific, territorially circumscribed, national space—and its idea. It therefore also helps us to gain a perspective on the astonishing fact that the reception of the United States on the global stage was virtually reversed only a few months after 2001. People around the world protested the US administration's blundering war against Afghanistan, the bloody war and failed occupation in Iraq, the refusal of the US administration to heed the wishes and procedures of the United Nations—indeed the deliberate humiliation of that body—and Washington's unilateralism in the economic, political, social, and environmental spheres. If there is a rogue state on the loose, a broad global consensus seemed to conclude, it is America's Bush administration. Even in Britain, the main ally of the United States in this period, a majority of people saw the United States as a greater threat to global peace than Al Qaeda.

In an extraordinary reversal of global public opinion, "We are all Americans" morphed quickly into an outright global opposition to the Bush administration's arrogant unilateralism. Virtually in unison, reporters and politicians chose to interpret such rising criticism of the administration and its war policies as anti-Americanism. "Aren't we the good guys, the world's saviors?" was the implied tone of faux innocence. A popular howl was raised against the Germans, Russians and especially the French, and at the nadir of this petulant, reactionary nationalism, French wine was poured down many an American sink while french fries became "freedom fries" in US Congress cafeterias.

That some deep-seated anti-Americanism did and does exist should not blind us to the convenient slippage by media and government confusing American government policy on the one side and America the people and the place on the other. Most people around the world are far more astute in making that distinction, and repugnance at the US war in Iraq is not the same as anti-Americanism. (The popular French response to freedom fries was whimsical, uncomprehending curiosity.) The cry of anti-Americanism in fact deflects global responsibility, provides a self-justifying refusal to comprehend US imperial complicity. This is the flip side of the deep personal identification many feel with "America" but manifestly not with the American state. The US behaving badly poses a visceral challenge to that affinity, and as with Vietnam, people around the world—much like many Americans themselves—feel that a warmongering US administration has betrayed them, taken "their" America from them.

There was nothing inevitable about the squandering of global magnanimity toward the US after 2001. But it was not unpredictable either, and its causes go much deeper than simply the reactionary pugilism of the Bush administration. A deep continuity connects US global ambition from the eighteenth to the twenty-first century, and it has helped to mold the long-term economic

and cultural as much as political policy of successive US administrations, Republican and Democratic alike. As I hope to show in
this book, the wars since 2001—in Palestine/Israel as much as
Afghanistan and Iraq, as well as older smoldering conflicts from
Colombia to Indonesia—should be seen less as moral crusades
against terrorism, and more as an expression of what I called at
the beginning "endgame global America," the culmination of a
US-centered (but *not exclusively American*) political and economic globalization. They represent the political face of globalization, leading to nothing less than a US-centered global
hegemony.

Put geographically, there is a trenchant contradiction between
on the one hand the global promise of a certain kind of
Americanism, to which people around the world can readily re-
late and invest in—the promise, and for no small few, the reality
of a comfortable life—and on the other hand the exclusionary,
elite and nationalist self-interest espoused as an integral part of
this Americanism. The latter represents a raft of global and simultaneously local practices that are experienced by millions
around the world (including many millions in the US itself) as
repressive, exploitative, vindictive, even life-threatening. US military repression, support for despotic regimes, unemployment,
and the poverty wages as well as dangerous work conditions experienced in many US multinational firms and their subsidiaries
and contractors are despised worldwide even as the dream of
America remains alive. For conservatives, this contradiction is
generally wished away. The reality of US-sponsored repression or
exploitation is either denied or excused as an exception to the
norm, or else it is justified as a pragmatic necessity for the defeat

of nefarious enemies: the American dream is cordoned off from reality. Liberals, by contrast, traditionally fold the contradiction into a narrative of realities versus ideals and focus on a moral parsing of specific events and episodes, sorting apart the regrettable failings of the ideal, the causes thereof and their implications. Wishing the contradiction into either the realm of human nature or that of philosophical inevitability, the liberal response too protects the ideal. The purpose of this book is to provide an alternative perspective, rooted in a historico-geographical reading of US global power and its contradictions.

The new sullen unilateralism of the US in global affairs also finds expression in US political economic strategy in the first years of the twenty-first century, but is not guided by any economic isolationism—far from it. Parallel with the war in Afghanistan and the violent occupation of Iraq, but rarely discussed in the same breath, the US government pursued global free trade policies as aggressively as, if not more so than, the preceding Clinton administration. The Clinton administration had mobilized the International Monetary Fund (IMF) to liberalize— deregulate and re-regulate—the financial sectors of economies across the world, eventually contributing to the so-called Asian economic crisis of 1997–1999. (The crisis was not restricted to Asia, of course, but produced economic tidal waves in Russia and Brazil and no economy was spared its ripples.) After 2000, the Bush administration, impatient with the calculated incrementalism of the Clinton globalists, sought more direct means of global economic dominance. They focused on dismantling import tariffs in other economies and challenging export subsidies on goods and services coming to the US. They used the World Trade

Organization (WTO) as the platform for this restructuring of the global economy, as well as regional agreements such as the Free Trade Areas of the Americas (FTAA), which would encompass thirty-four out of thirty-five western hemisphere economies (in a fit of protracted cold war revanchism, the US explicitly excluded Cuba). Couched in the language of freedom, equality and rights, these measures and agreements were actually proposed on terms heavily favorable to US economic interests. They were aimed, bluntly, at opening up the world economy for exploitation while maintaining the privileged position of the world's largest economy. By focusing on imports and exports, for example, the US government left subsidies to domestic producers—as opposed to exporters and importers—largely intact. This of course is the favored mechanism of US, European, and Japanese trade subsidies, and nowhere is this more so than in the agricultural sector, where the US subsidizes farmers to the tune of more than $300 billion annually. Military, textile, electronics, and high tech industries are similarly subsidized.

The cynicism and hypocrisy of this approach was evident for all to see. But US ruling interests still blithely forced it onto the agenda, using its arsenal of diplomatic and economic blackmail tools to move it forward. And in the immediate wake of post-9/11 sympathy, few wanted to challenge the US directly. When the world eventually balked and favorable agreements were not forthcoming, however, the US government responded with outright trade tariffs—30 percent against imported steel, much of it from Brazil, and even higher tariffs against selected European Union agricultural products—while continuing to hector the world about the sanctity of free trade. China ground trade talks to a stalemate, and Europe reciprocated with tariffs against US goods while mouthing the same free trade rhetoric. Emboldened and threatened by anti-globalization and global social justice movements at home, the leaders of twenty-two countries, including Brazil, South Africa, and India, trounced US-authored agricultural proposals at the 2003 Cancun summit. As the world pushed back, the WTO again and again rebuffed the US, which increasingly retreated to regional and bilateral agreements. Even in its own backyard, US plans for the FTAA were scuttled as the other nations of the hemisphere, meeting in Miami then Monterrey, refused to ratify the slanted proposals. An isolated United States was left, by early 2004, to plead rather pathetically for a revival of global trade talks, much as it had had to return to the United Nations, tail between legs, to plead for financial, personnel, and institutional support in the occupation and reconstruction of war-torn Iraq. Once again, this time in economic terms, a supposedly universal Americanism—"we are the world"—ran headlong into a narrow American nationalism, constituted as much from the outside as from the inside.

A liberal reading might frame this contemporary history as simply a contest between dual poles of nationalism and globalism. But that would miss the point. In the economic sphere as in the political, the crucial argument is that global ambition is constitutively nationalist, and by corollary, American nationalism is founded on globalist claims. That many other non-US influences also sculpt the politics, economics and cultures of globalization—from Japanese business practices to Bollywood movies to the political power of the European Union—is indisputable. Globalization may be American-led but it is manifestly not the same thing as Americanization. It is important to make this caveat up front, and we shall follow up these issues below, yet insofar as American nationalism infuses the arteries of a globalizing capitalism like no other, it is also crucial to follow further the contradiction of an American nationalism coiled within contemporary globalism. The Stars and Stripes draped briefly on Saddam's head in fact tells a longer historical and broader geographical story of global ambition.

New American Century, New Imperialism?

More than any other institution, the "Project for a New American Century" (PNAC) embodies this contradiction of class power claiming global sway yet national particularity. Established in 1996, PNAC later became a generative think tank for the younger Bush's administration. It was the brainchild of more than two dozen doctrinaire conservatives who felt that Bill Clinton's neoliberalism was too soft for US global ambition. Almost flippant in their periodic issuance of statements, missives, and op-ed pieces in the late 1990s, PNAC was forceful in its effort to move the national foreign policy agenda toward a more pugnacious conservatism. As such, PNAC saw itself in many ways as an ideological counterpoint to established think tanks such as the Council on Foreign Relations. The latter was and is scrupulously internationalist and politically liberal in the sense that it includes an eclectic range of political opinions, from left to right, within a broader rubric of US self-interest in the world. PNAC, by contrast, is far narrower, promoting a strident nationalist globalism spawned from the neoconservative movement. As such, by a strange historical twist of political vocabulary, this also makes PNAC true heirs to eighteenth century Enlightenment liberalism. That twist of political vocabulary may cut against the accepted tapestry of twentieth century American assumptions, according to which liberalism and conservatism occupy opposite political poles, but a longer view questions and contextualizes that conventional wisdom. Unraveling these arguments will be a central theme of the second chapter.

According to their "Statement of Principles," PNAC seeks to "shape a new century favorable to American principles and interests." Much like British rationalizations a century earlier, their quest for "American global leadership" oozes with the haughty obligations of empire, albeit with a different geographical focus:

> we cannot safely avoid the responsibilities of global leadership or the costs that are associated with its exercise. America has a vital role in maintaining peace and security in Europe, Asia and the Middle East. If we shirk our responsibilities, we invite challenges to our fundamental interests. The history of the 20th century should have taught us that it is important to shape circumstances before they emerge, and to meet threats before they become dire. The history of this century should have taught us to embrace the cause of American leadership.

Their major inspiration is "a Reaganite policy of military strength and moral clarity," in which the United States can "build on the successes of this past century and ... ensure our security and our greatness in the next."[4]

A lot can be unpacked from this PNAC manifesto. In the first place, geographically, PNAC's global vision seems to bypass

sub-Saharan Africa and Latin America. The first is neglected, presumably, because in the world market it is effectively redlined,
ghettoized in the neocon worldview as a basket case beyond re-
demption. Latin America, by contrast, is omitted for the opposite
reason: it is simply assumed, even after the Monroe Doctrine has
long ceased to have any teeth in polite society, that the rest of the
Americas constitute a reliable if occasionally petulant backyard to
US interests. That leaves Europe, Asia, and the Middle East, and it
is there that American power will make history. In the second
place, historically, PNAC clearly revives publisher Henry Luce's
1941 clarion call that the United States take global power simply
because it can. The future was "befogged" because despite its
power, the US was reluctant to use it. We should "accept whole-
heartedly our duty and our opportunity as the most powerful and
vital nation in the world," Luce said, "and in consequence to exert
upon the world the full impact of our influence, for such purposes as we see fit and by such means as we see fit."[5] If the cold
war frustrated that cherished desire, PNAC, seeing the cold war
won, yearns to resuscitate it.

Third, returning to the contradiction at the core of contemporary US imperialism, the global ambition of the framers of
the PNAC strategy is extraordinarily intertwined with a nationalist vision: the geographical slippage of national to global and
back again is greased with a language of national responsibility
for the global. By "shirking responsibilities," weak leaders not
only invite attacks on the US but contribute to global mayhem
and destabilization. If the British Empire accrued colonies in a
fit of absent-mindedness, as one famous apology for imperialism put it, PNAC's America must also, for the world's good,

become a reluctant imperialist. Global duty and obligation trump selfish reluctance.

PNAC's imprimatur shaped the Bush administration strategy from the start but thoroughly dominated it after September 11th. Many of their personnel were Reagan holdovers whose only critique of that era was that its conservatism remained stuck in the bubble gum of liberal sentiment. Among the PNACers who came to populate the younger Bush's administration were Vice President Dick Cheney (a Bush Sr. insider and previous Halliburton CEO), Donald Rumsfeld (Secretary of Defense), and Paul Wolfowitz (Deputy Secretary of Defense). Jeb Bush (Florida Governor, presidential brother, and co-engineer of George W. Bush's 2000 electoral victory) was also a signatory. Even more striking than the morphing of PNAC into the Bush administration is their insistence as early as 1997 on a pre-emptive strike against Iraq. It is "important to shape circumstances before they emerge, and to meet threats before they become dire," they observed.

PNAC and the neocon "revolution" it symbolizes are often seen as the cutting edge of a new American imperialism. While many in their ranks embrace empire without apology, the pejorative implications of "imperialism" may be less welcome. But since power for neocons is naked and transparent and their global calculation tilts toward the geopolitical, this only fortifies the sense of a new imperialism. To parse the difference between empire and imperialism is in any case to split hairs. Like the old imperialism, the new vision depends on a specific prescription for historical continuity and discontinuity. The fruition of US power represents the continuity in this vision: the new American century will be like the old except better, complete, a pure crystallization of legitimate power. The mistakes of the past will be corrected, American power—knocking on the door for the past century—will be unselfconsciously deployed, and the role of the US as world policeman will be accepted with honor and pride rather than embarrassed half-heartedness. The discontinuity of the vision is already implicit in this continuity: the delusions of the past—neoliberal incrementalism and global compromise, a certain penchant for reconciling global conflicts diplomatically rather than militarily—are all eschewed in this unbridled ambition for a forceful American globalism. Might, again, makes right. The rise of the influential neocons created a pervasive sense of discontinuity between the Bush government and the preceding Clinton administration: neoconservatism has taken over from neoliberalism as a foundational global strategy. Clinton's liberal internationalism is replaced by a much flintier nationalism. A willingness to work through international agreements, treaties, institutions and protocols—the UN, Kyoto environmental accord, International Criminal Court, Durban race summit—is replaced by an authoritarian unilateralism. There is no denying that these kinds of shifts mark the first years of the twenty-first century, but it is not immediately obvious how significant a historical discontinuity they will come to represent.

An old socialist saw has it that bourgeois democracy is a system whereby every four years the working class gets to vote for someone out of the ruling class. Nevertheless, the respective class bases of Bill Clinton's and George Bush's power were somewhat different. The right wing hatred of Clinton had everything to do with the fact that this Arkansas social climber was not to the ruling class born, and that having climbed the class ladder he provided a new model of Democratic rather than Republican populism. Yet the old socialist saw is not wrong. The Clinton administration's power was thoroughly rooted in fairly blue blood—financial capital and Wall Street—and as such it gave pure expression to a globalism innate to that sector of capital. In its geographical philandering, finance capital takes the global as its rightful stage of conquest. Accordingly, the Clinton Treasury Department under Robert Rubin enjoyed unprecedented influence and arguably represented the most powerful cabinet seat. A certain homology pertained, in other words, between the class basis of Clinton's power and a global neoliberalism that sought to establish, deregulate, and open up financial as well as commodity markets.

By contrast, the social basis of Bush-Cheney power lay in a somewhat different faction of the ruling class. The list of companies benefitting from the multi-billion dollar publicly funded rebuilding of Iraq—including but not restricted to Dick Cheney's Haliburton as well as Bechtel—or the secret list of companies meeting with Cheney to design tax-funded corporate welfare for energy capitalists suggests the class shift that occurred with the accession of that administration. The latter's social power pivots on the nexus between energy and the military and is rooted not in financial capital as such but in corporate capital devoted to the production of oil, energy equipment, armaments, aeronautics, military hardware and so forth. Its first Treasury Secretary, Paul O'Neill, came not from the financial sector but from Alcoa, a mining, manufacturing, and energy corporation, but the Treasury Department under Bush was marginalized and even O'Neill was treated with disdain and soon forced to resign.[6]

There are of course many interlinkages between the financial and productive wings of the capitalist class, between Wall Street and Houston or Los Angeles. Without industry producing commodities for profit, Wall Street would have nothing to invest, while producers in turn need Wall Street to float their stocks, issue credit, bankroll corporate takeovers, and so forth. Densely interlocking directorates weave these sectors together, and globalization, widely if not accurately conceived as emanating from the financial sector, is just as much about the international reorganization and expansion of commodity production. For all their connections, however, the pursuit of industrial profit involves different kinds of calculation from the pursuit of interest on capital lent. And so it is not surprising that administrations whose power is rooted in different factions of the capitalist class wield global power and express their global ambitions somewhat differently. The significance of this distinction becomes clear in the larger historical and economic context.

As theorists from Marx to Schumpeter and Kondratieff to Kuznets have argued, capitalist expansion is highly cyclical. For Johns Hopkins sociologist Giovanni Arrighi, these "systemic cycles" exhibit a clear geo-historical pattern. Cycles of economic expansion built on the production of commodities—material and immaterial—gradually morph into economies where the greatest concentration of paper profit comes from the financial rather than industrial sector. The reasons for this are complex but not especially mysterious. Long cycles of investment in the productive sectors heighten competition and produce low-cost competitors, leading eventually to lower profit rates. Yet to the extent they are successful in the global market, national economies garner

larger and larger quantities of capital in search of investment possibilities, and the tendency is to make more and more of the return by financial rather than productive means—by lending to
others rather than directly investing oneself. Interest on lent capital increasingly replaces industrial profit. Arrighi observes this
movement in prior historical moments, most recently at the end
of the nineteenth century when the economies of Britain, France,
and the United States all experienced an extraordinary shift of
power away from industrial toward finance capital.[7] The era of
the robber barons was supplanted by the power of the House of
Morgan, the Rothschilds, and the Bank of England.

Yet this centralization of power in financial capital was momentary, receding with war and extinguished in depression, not
to gain such heights again till the end of the twentieth century.
Moreover, and more ominously in the present context, the rise of
financial power was accompanied by a geographical shift in un-
derlying economic power. While Britain consolidated financial
power after the 1890s, becoming the world's bank—a rentier
state—its financial hegemony actually marked the zenith of its
imperialism; competitors, especially the US and Germany, supplanted its economic power. Decline was not instantaneous, but
the sun began to set on the British Empire. As one theorist of imperialism put it at the time, a "rentier state is a state of parasitic,
decaying capitalism."[8]

The quite different policies of the Clinton and Bush administrations should be considered against a parallel history of the fortunes of productive vis-à-vis finance capital in the US since the
1970s, and the question of whether the ascent of Bush and the
neocons represents a new imperialism should be treated

accordingly. Where the Clinton administration was centrally concerned about geo-economic power—the power to control the myriad institutions and activities that orchestrate the global market—the language of power since 9/11 has been all about geography. Oil is clearly a central calculation in the decision to invade Iraq and topple the Saddam Hussein regime, but as many have remarked, its relevance goes well beyond Iraq or simply the control of supplies for the US market. With the second highest declared reserves in the world, Iraq becomes a pawn in US competition with Europe and Japan and increasingly China. By the same token, the militarization of post-Soviet southwest Asia—Azerbaijan, Uzbekistan, Kazakhstan—is part of a struggle to control the supply of large oil reserves from this region. The new US pugilism, inspired by a political subclass with their social base in the energy/military sector of the capitalist class, can be seen as a strategy for enhanced US control of global oil supply over the next two or three decades vis-à-vis competitors.[9] To the extent that such a strategy succeeded, the US would enjoy unparalleled global economic hegemony.

In his classic analysis, Lenin located the origins of imperialism in the competitive logic of capitalism and the monopoly power, especially rooted in finance capital, that this created. This was a brutal and despicable process for Lenin but not without a silver lining insofar as the centralization of capital might pave the way for a broader socialization of power. It is now clear that imperialism was not "the highest stage of capitalism," and contemporary imperialism sports some different features from earlier forms. Where Lenin posited a close relationship between monopoly capital, especially finance capital, and the nation-state, that connection is significantly weakened today under the aegis of transnational capital. Lenin was surely correct to reject the territorial fetish of his contemporary, the "renegade" Karl Kautsky, and yet Kautsky, raising the possibility of some kind of "superimperialism," looks prescient today. Where Lenin thought that inter-imperialist rivalries led inevitably to war, as indeed they did in 1914, Kautsky thought a coalition of imperialist states might fashion a relatively stable global rule among themselves in pursuit of global economic plunder. That has not happened, but present-day US unilateralism does raise the possibility that Kautsky may have been half right, anticipating the prospect of a US "superimperialism." Where Lenin did turn out to be extraordinarily prescient is in his distinction between imperialism and colonialism. Imperialism, for Lenin, was not simply a land grab of the colonial sort but a logical result of capitalist competition working through a system of national states. Hence his focus on finance capital; colonialism was at best a means of imperialism, but there were others. Where many on the left have not yet embraced this insight, and still treat colonialism and imperialism as the same phenomenon, the neocons who have embraced empire are in this respect at least the truer Leninists.

This latter point, especially, suggests considerable historical continuity rather than discontinuity with the past, and it should suggest that today's imperialism may not be so new. Whatever the tactical discrepancies between the Clinton and Bush administrations, neoliberals and neoconservatives, they share entirely the larger goal of an American globalism, and this was never clearer than in the inability of presidential candidate John Kerry to distinguish himself from George W. Imperialism today takes some new forms compared with the colonial era, but its economic and political integument is fairly continuous over the past century. Viewing empire through geographical lenses helps to crystallize that continuity: although the location of imperial power may have switched from London to New York and Washington, and although a territorially defined colonialism may have given way to an imperialism of markets and missiles, and although the national definition of capitals may have given way to a new globalism, the reality of exploitation and domination of the poorest parts of the world by the richest and most powerful has not changed at all. In that sense the wars of the first years of the twenty-first century are all about a resurgent imperialism. For all that war in Iraq has to do with oil, therefore, it is not simply a war for oil but a larger war to control the global economic infrastructure, practices and relations that orchestrate the global economy (of which oil is a significant part). In short, it is about the endgame of globalization.

The draping of the US flag over the doomed statue of Saddam Hussein in 2003 expressed precisely the ambitions of this resurgent imperialism as well as its contradictions. Simultaneously a symbol of nationalist power and—insofar as it stood for the victory of a supposed international coalition—a sign of global ambition, the humiliating flagging of Saddam exposed the geographical slippage between national and global scale claims. This contradiction lies at the heart of American imperialism and although it has become a hallmark of America's global profile during the so-called American century, its roots lie in an earlier formative period of US power in the world.

It is a central argument of this book that American imperial ambition is not new either with the neocons or the post-cold war world but that it has been episodic throughout US history. The first truly *global* (as opposed to international) assertion of US power came in the years following 1898 and leading up to World War I. A second episode came with the culmination of World War II. In this context, the Clinton and Bush administrations represent two sides of a single historical moment, namely the zenith of a third moment of US global ambition. In victory and defeat, both were committed to a successful endgame of globalization.

LIBERALISM AND THE

ROOTS OF AMERICAN

GLOBALISM

... a remarkable force: this fixed, dogmatic liberalism of a
liberal way of life.

Louis Hartz, 1955

Liberalism in the latter part of the twentieth century was
broadly seen to be progressive, on the right side of history.
Liberals opposed the cold war and imperialism, were against
racism, reviled oppression, and saw themselves as marking
progress beyond a stodgy, heartless, out-of-date conservatism;
they supported social welfare for the poor, feminism and civil
rights, self-rule for colonial peoples, environmental politics,
even—within limits—unions. They supported individual liberties and social equality, opposed corporate capital when it over-

stepped its bounds, and generally believed in government regulations against the predations of a capitalist market when it threatened to run amuck. Above all else, liberalism was pitted against a
conservatism that seemed to defend the rights of established
class, race, and gender power. Liberalism opposed both a feudalism that preceded it and a fascism and communism that arose at
different moments on the same watch.

This slant on liberalism took its cue from the evolution of a
specifically American politics in the twentieth century, but powerful as it was, it was not the only take on liberalism. When people in Latin America and Europe began to recognize as
"neoliberal" the global economic policies of the Thatcher, Kohl
and Reagan-Bush governments, their successors, and the World
Bank and IMF in the 1980s and 1990s, they conjured up a much
longer, deeper and broader tradition of liberalism than recent
US definitions encompass. They recognized the connections between post-1970s global economic ideologies extolling the
global marketplace and the social and intellectual revolutions of
the seventeenth and eighteenth centuries that ushered in a new
political economy of bourgeois property rights, market power,
and the rule of national states. This "classical liberalism," they
perceived, was often integral with, rather than antagonistic to,
latter day conservatism, and neoliberalism deliberately harkened
back to that classical tradition.

The gestalt of a narrow, elite, national self-interest which, when
twisted slightly in the light, reveals a truculent globalism of universal rights, liberties, and justice, characterizes contemporary
neoliberalism and neconservatism alike. Both are fruit of the classical liberal tradition. Beautifully symbolized by the draping of

the Stars and Stripes over the toppling head of Saddam Hussein, this gestalt also marks the history of the American Empire since 1898 and has deep roots in the intellectual and practical origins of the United States and its subsequent expansion. Philosophically this takes us back to the Enlightenment, the origins of modern liberalism, and the ideas enshrined in what is strangely referred to as the "new nation." In truth, of course, the United States of America is one of the oldest national states, predating for example Italy and Germany by almost a century. (That the long pre-national histories of the latter have been morphed into contemporary national memory and made to stand as figures of an almost infinite national past—weren't the Romans Italians?—only points to the extent to which the European founders of the United States largely obliterated existing histories and humanities across the New World in order to make a "new nation.") But the Enlightenment is the central key here to understanding US globalism before globalization: in the founding of the United States it finds a more faithful practical and political expression than in any other territory of the globe, the Scottish Enlightenment and the French Revolution notwithstanding.

Liberalism, Enlightenment, Americanism

When viewed outside the twentieth century American box, liberalism is not the antithesis of contemporary conservatism but its political backbone. Such a liberalism harkens back to the revolutionary bourgeois political economy of Adam Smith, Kant's cosmopolitanism, the willed reason of Rousseau, Hume's practical

empiricism, and of course John Locke's juridical politics of property and rights. All contributed in various permutations to the
"new nation," but as many have suggested, Lockean liberalism in
particular is carved into the grooves of the US Constitution. "In
the beginning all the world was *America*," Locke once wrote, giving biblical blessing to an entrepreneurial liberalism that more
than returned the compliment to the English philosopher. The
enshrinement of the juridical individual as variously property
owner, man in the market, bearer of specified rights, and appro-
priator of nature took no purer practical form than in the documents of America's national birth. Nor were they anywhere put to
more judicious use. This gave rise to what political theorist Louis
Hartz, in his classic *The Liberal Tradition in America*, called "natural liberalism"—an appeal to liberty, equality, and freedom that
rooted its claims in a philosophy of natural rights supposedly
common to all mankind.[1]

The revolutionary success of this classical liberalism lay in its
extension of such rights beyond the narrow, absolutist confines of
feudal, monarchial, and aristocratic power—its simultaneous
embrace and enablement of bourgeois democracy. It provided a
progressive answer to Hobbes's withering judgment that absolutist government was the necessary price if the precipitous anarchy of natural selfishness was to be kept in check. Where Locke
was occupied by legal contract, Adam Smith stressed the extraordinary unseen work of the market, which not only capitalized on
individual freedoms—literally—and organized for the provision
of mass needs, but did so in such a way that the overall interests of
the commonweal were supposedly safeguarded and advanced.
From pins to people, the new capitalist market made the world go

round. Revolutionary bourgeois freedom in the market cogged with Locke's freedoms in the world of law and jurisprudence. With Kant's more enigmatic aspirations for cosmopolitan citizenship in the background, Locke and Smith together provided twin intellectual inspirations for a series of interlocked beliefs that anchored the political flowering of capitalism and the self-understanding of emerging bourgeois society and its individualism. A society of individual property owners, free and independent before the law and with equal recourse to it, who met in the competitive marketplace, and who enjoyed the right to a democratic vote and voted unashamedly in their own self interest—such a society, the Enlightenment promised, would produce the best outcome for everyone. This vision was not uncontested: its individualism was always tempered by the republican drive for a workable state; day-to-day revolt was inspired less by Locke or Smith than by taxes, oppressive law, and aristocratic foible; and Tom Paine's "rights of man" aside, Enlightenment liberalism was adopted as a rationale for revolution after, as much as before, the fact.[2] Still, its promise did spark, fuel, and stoke the colonial revolt against a European power that was too slowly casting off its absolutism.

Nor was this a vision without contradiction. The class, race, and gender contours of this bourgeois political landscape are now well understood: Kant's cosmopolitan geography and anthropology included some pretty awful racist denigrations of much of humanity, and Rousseau's exultation of reason presumed it a distinctly European possession. Adam Smith's civic heroes were entrepreneurs with everyone else playing bit parts. The original citizens of the US were property owners and almost exclusively men. Slaves counted as three-fifths of a person for purposes of property-owning political arithmetic (they obviously couldn't vote), and they were generally held by men who were indistinguishable in many ways from the aristocracies across the water—aristocracies which, it has to be said, at least had the decency (under political pressure from the bourgeoisie) to abolish slavery decades in advance of the United States. Native Americans counted for nothing at all: they were beyond the pale, to invoke a political-geographical image from a British imperium that America believed it was transcending. Locke was especially decisive in this context. The taking of "common lands" found in the "state of nature" is justified, he said, insofar as its subsequent working—the mixing of labor with nature—produces profit for the common good. That previous users of the land could be excluded from the commonweal via the logic that they themselves were part of the state of nature simply reaffirmed the vision.

The interlocking of liberalism and nationalism in the forging of America is not a seamless fit. Philosopher Omar Dahbour argues forcefully that resorting to a definition of political community at the national scale attenuates a series of contradictions at the heart of liberalism but in no way resolves them.[3] Who precisely belongs to this national community accorded liberal rights by the state? Where are its boundaries? For non-citizens, how are partial rights of citizenship determined? Does liberalism have a theory of economic inclusion, economic citizenship? These conundrums are multifold but are more dramatically on display in the origins and evolution of the United States than in any other instance. Liberalism is "a doctrine which everywhere in the West has been a glorious symbol of individual liberty," writes Louis Hartz, "yet in America its compulsive power has been so great that it has posed a threat to liberty itself." How could liberalism become a threat to liberty? For Dahbour, the inherent illiberalism of the liberal tradition crystallizes in its historical, geographical and political minuet with nationalism. A liberalism that takes the juridical individual as its primary element finds it impossible, ultimately, to reconcile with the priority accorded territorial oneness, national collectivity, and communal identity presupposed by the nation-state. For Hartz, too, the answer also lies in the bowels of liberalism itself. Locke harbors "a hidden conformitarian germ to begin with, since natural law tells equal people equal things, but when this germ is fed by the explosive force of modern nationalism, it mushrooms into something pretty remarkable."[4] (This liberal critique is today a centerpiece of conservatism: when the same "conformitarian germ" is enforced by the state, as in affirmative action, egalitarianism itself becomes oppressive.)

Remarkable indeed. Nothing is more insidious than the liberal fain of equality between people who are demonstrably and desperately unequal. There is little liberal victory in the fact that Bill Gates has the same right to apply for workfare as an unemployed single parent. Neither in the market nor in court is a homeless mother the equal of George Bush. Those who resurrected the notion of neoliberalism in the 1980s to describe the economic policies of corporate globalization—centered in New York, Tokyo, and London—understood precisely this "hidden conformitarian germ" masquerading as "natural law." Adam Smith's law of the market was re-anointed on the throne of global common sense (Hume) and the greed for profit was restored to its position as a natural urge (Hobbes); in the meantime people's basic needs for food, water, and shelter were relegated to the pleadings of special interest groups. Conformity was no natural germ but the goal of raw power at the global scale. Opponents of corporate globalization were written off as trying to stem the natural tide of capital or worse, as terrorists against all things American.

Writing in the poisonous political caldron of the 1950s cold war, and with a clear target in his sights, Hartz—himself a radical liberal who wanted to salvage the promise of liberalism, however contradictory—ventured that whatever its ideological power, liberalism in its original sense had never actually been put into practice. Nationalism blocked the path. Even in the United States, he concluded, there "has never been a 'liberal movement' or a real 'liberal party'": "we have only had the American way of life, a nationalist articulation of Locke which usually does not know that Locke himself is involved." The unanimity of Americanism, widely associated today with a conservative mission, is by Hartz's account the product of liberalism *par excellence*, "the bizarre fulfillment of liberalism."[5]

The liberal tradition itself has internalized parts of this critique, at times spurning an implausible nationalism in favor of a more politically correct internationalism yet at the same time remaining firmly attached to Americanism. This goes to the heart of the contradiction of US global power in the twenty-first century. It describes not simply the hoary old dualism of nationalism versus internationalism, itself a liberal nostrum. Rather, the best of this modern liberalism remains true to Kant insofar as it combines an ambitious universalism—Kant's cosmopolitanism—with the unassailable imprimatur of its American lineage.

American exceptionalism—the belief that the US is different from and special compared to other nations—only represents an alternative expression of this contradiction: America would and should take its model liberalism to the world, safe in the conceit that the world needs and wants it; but exceptionalism always provides the resort back into a narrower sense of national victimization should the world spurn its advances.

Liberal American internationalism today, therefore, is red, white, and blue nationalist at the same time, thoroughly co-dependent on a narrow nationalism—liberal or otherwise. It thrives by consuming nationalism much as a python swallows a pig. The devoured pig of one nationalism sustains it for a while but it must eventually go hunting for more of the same. To the extent that liberal internationalism is not periodically fed by nationalism, it will waste away and die.

Congeries of Liberalism and Empire

So how do we account for the constellation of ideas that pass for popular American liberalism in the twentieth century—liberalism as a synonym for a left social politics irrevocably opposed to conservatism? The historical geography of liberalism provides the first clues to the answer. Outside the United States the liberal tradition *per se* either disintegrated in the cauldron of twentieth-century wars and ideological struggles or else, where kept alive (as in Canada, Britain, or Australia), remained—however much transformed from the eighteenth century—a conservative tradition. In the United States, by contrast, twentieth-century liberalism moved dramatically to the left, so much so that it indeed became a synonym for a left-leaning politics. This happened for very specific reasons that have everything to do with disparate worldwide responses to the socialist challenge of the late nineteenth century and first third of the twentieth century.

Throughout the nineteenth century in Europe and North America, an ascendant liberalism provided the banner for the bourgeois classes but found itself challenged between the remnants of a fading monarchial power on one side and the gathering strength of working class movements and organizations on the other. Occasionally these struggles bubbled over: in 1848 throughout Europe, in 1870–1871 on the Rhine and in Paris, or around the world between 1917 and 1919. Revolutionary communist organizations pupated out of these movements, and they in turn threw up a social democratic response—most typically a labor or socialist parliamentary party—which while solidly rooted in working class politics and even Marxist ideas, sought non-revolutionary means to express many working class people's political aspirations. Liberals found themselves squeezed between the new politics and the old, and their response to this challenge was neither uniform nor consistent. That said, it did have a pattern. A certain liberal reformism in the late nineteenth century simultaneously reasserted its eighteenth century roots and gravitated toward the petit bourgeoisie—rural or urban—as an alternative to the old aristocracy on one side and the social democrats on the other. Liberalism remade itself between the twin poles of Toryism and social democracy.

It was different in the United States, however. There, despite the power of unions and working class organizations and despite

Eugene Debs' polling a million socialist votes in 1912, the social democratic tradition never gained enough support to institutionalize itself in national politics. Social democracy was sufficiently suppressed that it was unable to achieve what it did elsewhere, namely the co-option of working class revolt into the grooves of parliamentary bureaucracy. It fell to liberalism, emerging from a thoroughly patrician progressivism, to perform this task, to transform itself into the antidote to socialism. Originally the fresh ideology of a blossoming global capitalism, the liberal tradition was now put to work in a more defensive role which in turn transformed it. Woodrow Wilson, a devout liberal yet arch-conservative at the same time, was the practical and symbolic fulcrum of this transformation. A scourge of the monopoly trusts in the early days of the twentieth century yet also a single-minded warrior against socialism, Wilson more than anyone pioneered the transformation of liberalism into a left-leaning immune-system against socialism in America.

American liberalism, in other words, remade itself to fulfil the task that social democracy fulfilled elsewhere. It became a progressive force, absorbing yet dampening the leftward impulse of socialism; it was willing to burn the toes of capital in order to keep feeding the larger body. It largely lived out the agenda Wilson established, a liberalism quite at home with racism and class exploitation, yet one which responded when necessary to political pressure (as in the granting of female suffrage). Liberalism expanded into a bipolar role of co-opting any progressive urge among the multiracial working class while also viciously repressing that same force when it organized too much of a challenge to the power of capital or the liberal state. This incarnation of liberalism presented its truest colors during and after World War I when Wilson, while fighting Senate conservatives to establish a League of Nations, was also fighting socialists in the street, organizing repressive detentions against workers, organizers, and immigrants, and deporting American "reds" to Russia. (His administration had already handed down a ten-year sentence on Eugene Debs for delivering an anti-war speech.) Such a liberalism had a resurgence in World War II when Wilson's spiritual successor, Franklin Roosevelt, mulling over plans for a supposedly progressive United Nations, despised by American conservatives, also suppressed wartime strikes with an iron fist and imprisoned 120,000 Japanese Americans in concentration camps.

One could think of this as an exceptional American history—only in America did liberalism take such an ideological and contradictory leftward turn—but that would be a mistake. The story of American liberalism's twentieth-century tilt to the left makes sense only in the context of a United States vociferously located at the heart of global affairs. The most surprising aspect of this may be that the cultural-political power of the United States was sufficient to export the US experience into a widespread synonymity of liberalism with the left. If twentieth century American liberalism did not immediately co-opt the left around the world, it did make inroads, and over the long term ground down the opposition. It took the end of the cold war to make this happen. When in the 1980s the old elite liberal party in Britain, with its decaying power based in the rural *petit bourgeoisie*, entered a coalition with social democratic defectors from the Labour Party, they participated in a practical redefinition of liberalism that in many ways aped the US experience decades earlier. The new Liberal

Democratic Party explicitly positioned itself between the heartless toryism of Margaret Thatcher and the last gasps of working class parliamentary socialism represented by union power and the Labour Party. That the subsequent Labour leader Tony Blair effectively joined this tide and became among the most neo of liberals in the 1990s only reaffirms the point.

Opponents of neoliberalism were therefore astute in branding the rightward shift of the 1980s with this name, even if the range of adherents it attracted was wide and versatile. Tony Blair may have been bosom buddies with Bill Clinton, but he went to war as lap dog for George W. Bush. At home, he also finished off the anti-welfare state work of Thatcher in a way that she could never have accomplished, much as Clinton's welfare reforms of 1996 completed the work of 1980s Republicanism—Reaganism on steroids. Whatever the fights over Iraq in 2003, Blair's "New Labour" and Gerhard Schröder's "Die neue Mitte" connected not just to Clintonian ideology but to George Bush's flintier conservatism aimed at recentering the capitalist market as arbiter of social survival and success. Neoliberalism filled the political vacuum in the wake not so much of liberalism per se (the US and perhaps Canada excepted) but of its social democratic variant, which had largely lost its class base. However abrasive and conservative some of its recent US proponents may be, the new neoliberalism does not represent an alternative to a heady but short-lived neoconservatism but rather the cocoon within which the latter was nurtured, however briefly.

In this context, the blossoming of neoliberalism around the world in the 1990s is nothing short of remarkable. It grabbed Russia and eastern Europe by the throat as an accompaniment to capitalist reconstruction; reconquered German social democracy from its timid postwar survival; impressed itself on Asian and Latin American elites both through the blandishments of the World Bank and IMF and the self-interested proclivities of local elites with an economics training in Chicago, London, Cambridge (Massachusetts), or Tokyo. That neoliberalism is thoroughly conservative—again pinning its banner to the sanctity of property, the market, and state-mandated individualism (and the wealthier the individual the more sacrosanct the individualism)—is not a paradox but precisely the point. Subsequent to its eighteenth century assemblage, enshrined in the US Constitution, liberalism became a conservative artifact throughout most of the world, so much so that even in the United States, turn-of-the-twentieth-century aristocrats, perhaps best represented by Henry Adams and his brother Brooks, railed against the Constitution precisely for its "fixed, dogmatic liberalism," as Louis Hartz put it. The reinvention of an anomalous left-wing liberalism in the US in the twentieth century has, quite ironically, paved the way for a global rediscovery of some of the basic tenets of liberalism as the conservatism of capitalism *par excellence*.

For the social liberalism that arose in the United States in the twentieth century, empire and imperialism were anathema. Yet by the late 1990s it was not just neconservatives but—and more to the point—neoliberals who came to embrace the notion of an American empire. Recognizing that the new twenty-first century American empire relied on overwhelming military as well as economic, political, and cultural power rather than immediate territorial control (colonialism), political scientist and journalist Michael Ignatieff openly embraced empire and enthusiastically endorsed the Iraq war. This was widely seen as a shocking admission—liberals outing themselves as pro-war, worse, pro-empire!—but it simply represented an historical reconnection to liberal roots.[6] In retrospect, twentieth-century American liberalism was a convenient and highly functional aberration from the main course, one that justified the global ambition of US capital. It may have been rhetorically opposed to empire via the self-serving confusion of imperialism and colonialism, which seemed to let US global ambition off the hook, but this liberalism was itself the architect of empire.

Liberals have traditionally endorsed empire. They have occupied the forefront of imperial ambition, and the current Washington neoliberals—spanning both parties—resemble no one more than their nineteenth-century British predecessors. Political scientist Uday Mehta goes back to the origins of British liberalism and finds that "it is liberal and progressive thinkers" in the eighteenth and nineteenth century who "endorse the empire as a legitimate form of political and commercial governance." Nineteenth-century European liberalism exhibited "a growing confidence in its universality and cosmopolitanism," much as we see today America's confidence in its own global reach. Reflecting on the translation of liberalism from Europe to the US, Mehta makes the point that "the radical edge to Locke's thought got severely eviscerated" and in fact "became the voice of a matter-of-fact conservatism." However that may be, this conservatism didn't simply meld liberal philosophy to imperial assertion but found the urge to empire inherent in liberalism from the start. To affirm this critique of historical liberalism, one does not have to embrace the conservatism of Edmund Burke, as Mehta seems to do.[7]

It is sufficient to highlight, as Mehta does superbly, the connection between liberalism and empire.

In philosophical terms, then, the slippage between narrow national self-interest and claims to represent global good and right emanate not simply from the Enlightenment but from the ways in which Enlightenment universalist ambition was put to work in the context of a specific national experiment. The founding documents and ideologies of the United States did not simply create a new model of national citizenship, the authority of which ended at the boundaries of the nation. They clearly did this but did a lot more besides. They also mobilized the "natural rights of man," loudly proclaimed as universal, into the particularity of an Americanism which placed itself not simply as geographical but global historical alternative to inherited forms of social oppression, exploitation, and inequality. America was the future. As Louis Hartz's sympathetic critique suggests, the core contradiction between national particularity and global pretension was inoculated by a self-medicating liberalism that took itself as "natural" and by definition, therefore, above reproach.

As the vestigial political lies that kindled the Iraq war became increasingly public, multiplying daily on TV screens and newspaper headlines, and as the personal, political, and economic costs of the Iraq war soared with little prospect of an end—more than 1,000 US troops and up to 100,000 Iraqis dead and counting, with hundreds tortured, raped and killed in US jails—erstwhile liberals such as Michael Ignatieff came to the defense of war in particularly eighteenth-century, almost Hobbesian, terms: "To defeat evil, we may have to traffic in evils."[8] Rarely since 1898 has the vice of liberal American imperialism been so honestly on display. We should at least ask, given its complicity with imperialism, whether liberalism may itself be a greater evil compared to the alternatives.

Geographies of Practical Liberalism

Striding through the New World, liberal thought generalized and at the same time flattered itself as universal. It represented itself as an abstraction above the geographical and historical specificities of European imperial expansion. This is a point made sharply by Mehta, who recognizes that the liberal justification of empire was vitally enabled by the abstraction from territorial realities in particular. Put differently, the success—and the failure—of American liberalism rests in part on a "lost geography." This lost geography came to fruition in various guises, most recently in twentieth and early twenty-first century ideologies of globalization. As well, liberal universalism fueled a powerful depoliticization of global ambition in the popular imagination.[9] But the abstraction from space and time is in no way automatic, and Mehta's mistake concerning the apparent disregard of territorial questions in the nineteenth century may be to read the lost geographical sensibility of the twentieth back into the philosophy of the seventeenth and eighteenth centuries, or at least to assume that the fine philosophical proclamations of the Enlightenment lost little of their idealist abstraction as they were put to work in the westward expansion of the United States. But philosophy is all about such abstraction, and in practice, the abstraction from geographical (and historical) specificity is at best uneven and rarely consonant with the gritty daily geographies of American expansionism. The geography of liberalism in practice reveals a tremendous amount about the politics of globalization, past and present.

For the bright new liberalism of the nineteenth century, America was a geographical project *par excellence*—geography, not history, was destiny. History, a seemingly eternal litany of oppressions and intrigues sedimented one on top of the other, was thankfully left behind on another continent's Atlantic shore, while the landscape of North America provided a shining alternative, a challenge certainly, but more importantly a bounteous opportunity. The raw natural vistas of the New World came already imbued as a trinity of god, nature, and (Lockean) man, a brilliant opening rather than a closure. This is Jefferson, not only writing on Virginia, but organizing the Louisiana Purchase and sending Lewis and Clark up the Missouri and over to Oregon; it is Emerson's metaphysical sublime; it is painter Frederic Edwin Church's hallowed landscapes revealing a new continent bathed in heavenly light. Here lay a whole new "state of nature" available for use and possession by Adam Smith's entrepreneurs, guided by the divine principles of Lockean justice, their eyes on the prize of Kant's cosmopolitan promise—again, we are the world.

Geographical escape provided the foundation of liberal possibility in practice. But geography also offered something much more constructive. "During most of American history," writes Walter Russell Mead, "geography and demography united to proclaim that, all things being equal, the mere passage of time would make the United States increasingly richer, more powerful, and better respected in the world community." Here history is rendered abstract—the mere passage of time—while geography has an active voice, makes claims, reworks and gives substance to hopes and desires. And indeed geographical reason and rationality were forged and harnessed in support of this enterprise—geography was recast as a social and physical technology of empire. Although the claim would certainly raise eyebrows today, it should not be surprising in retrospect that during "the first six or seven decades of the nineteenth century," the search for geographical knowledge, broadly conceived, "dominated the sciences in America."[10] The practical geography of the new continent, as well as the geographical reasoning it both inspired and required, was not just integral but pivotal to the earliest ambitions for a globalization of European ambition in the new image of America.

Geography, of course, became destiny in a far darker sense. The liberal conquest of the North American continent was not bathed in quite such a heavenly light as Frederic Church's majestic paintings portrayed. Nor was the mixing of labor with nature devoid of horrors. Even as Church was painting, the waters of the expanding United States ran red with native blood, were being depleted of fish, canalized, and turned into open sewers for the effluent of capitalist industrialism. Farm lands were sucked of nutrient while forest lands were felled before the axe in anticipation of the same fate. The earth was gouged for coal and steel and other raw materials. The bounty of buffalo was plundered almost to extinction, numerous bird species extirpated. The end of the nineteenth century brought the final geographical solution to the centuries-long American social cleansing of its original inhabitants. The remnant minority who were not killed by war, disease, starvation, privation, or legalized army and settler violence were herded into rural ghettos called reservations, generally located on the most barren land, where jobs and services barely existed. Having been vilified as savages still in a "state of nature"—mere appurtenances of the land—they were vilified anew as hapless authors of their own geographical destiny. The enslavement of Africans as a labor force for this universalizing European liberalism rooted in the New World gave rise to a different if equally reprehensible geographical rupture in the name of civilized progress.

Nothing in these experiences contradicted Enlightenment liberalism; rather they built it out. The purported savagery of the native American population, noble or otherwise, and the inferiority of Africans only reaffirmed the freedom and equality of all the others considered "Man"—their inalienable rights and so forth. Excluded from citizenship and status as juridical individuals, yet "domestic in a foreign sense," as the Supreme Court would later put it, the social and territorial detention of Indians and African Americans in "free" America was the crude precursor for colonizations in Puerto Rico and Cuba, Hawaii, and the Philippines.

1898 was therefore neither a beginning nor an end of empire, as is variously argued. It neither initiated a period of empire that didn't previously exist, nor did it end an experience of empire that somehow ceased to exist in the new century. It did not separate the US from the European experience of colonialism but was rather continuous with it. America as continental expansion may have been the most successful colonialism of all time, and 1898 represented simultaneously its continental fulfillment and its serious commitment to trans-continental continuity. Yet the post-1898 world was simultaneously a denial of that specific form of colonialism. Neither an end nor a beginning, it was a transitional break. It provoked the political dilemma that bent twentieth century American liberalism in its own peculiar direction.

Prior to the economic depression of late 1893, it was evident to all that the US economy was producing profit and accumulating capital at a record rate. It had already surpassed a declining Britain, and Germany was the only competitor. Despite massive industrialization at home, only pockets of uncapitalized frontier land now remained in the US, and outlets for profitable investments of surplus capital were rapidly shrinking. Continued economic expansion beyond the confines of the continent was not only logical and necessary but quite consistent with the political claims registered from the origins of the Republic. From interventions in the Haitian revolution, the invasion of Canada, the proclamation of the Monroe Doctrine, and subsequent interventions in the Caribbean and Central America, not to mention the dismemberment of Mexico, the geography of US expansionism was never confined, ideologically or practically—neatly or otherwise—to what became circumscribed as the forty-eight states. The spurt of manly colonialism culminating in 1898 surely expressed a certain cultural impulse, a "surplus energy" inherent in the twinned projects of nation building and empire building as Amy Kaplan suggests,[11] but it just as surely provided the prospect of outlets for an overflowing economy that began powering itself out of crisis.

It was a short-lived colonialism, however, not because of some liberal American antipathy to empire—quite the opposite—nor because it solved the questions of economic and cultural expansionism. It was short-lived precisely because it *didn't* solve these problems. A *successful* colonialism would have been pursued. But by 1898, where else was there to go? Mexico, Canada, Japan, Russia, Venezuela, or Brazil? That these were recognized states, many of them republics (or in the case of Canada, a British dominion) with some degree of juridical sovereignty, did not at all prevent US intervention. But chasing Pancho Villa south of the border was one thing, colonizing the place quite another. The geographical reality was that, with few minor interstitial exceptions, the entire surface of the earth was already carved out by republics, states, and colonizing powers. Most of the colonies of 1898 had to be wrested away from a declining Spanish power, and few (if any) significant opportunities of this sort remained. Would the US really stand up to Britain militarily? Invade Brazil? Take on China? For all the pundits who pointed in this direction, others were more sober.

To the American ruling class, a territorially based imperialism seemed too difficult militarily, too costly economically, and potentially too damaging to the self-professed rhetoric of liberal democracy and the self-determination of peoples around the world. The likelihood of defeat at the hands of local opposition, an independent republic, a European power, or a combination of all three did not prevent some saber-rattling vis-à-vis East Asia and Latin America, and it by no means prevented further intervention—especially in the latter. But it did forestall subsequent colonialism (the Virgin Islands were *purchased* in 1916 from Denmark). A new means would have to be found. The answer was already at hand. US corporations and magnates were already investing in raw material extraction and even manufacturing in foreign lands, especially Monroe Doctrine countries where United

Fruit and W.R. Grace, rubber merchants and gun manufacturers, railroad companies and oil prospectors, not to mention the bankers who serviced them, could all depend on US gunboats to back up their investments. Certainly, investment in the colonies of European powers was harder due to tariffs and preferences, but there was also China. Just as Teddy Roosevelt's macho expression of "surplus energy" took him on hunting trips to British-controlled Africa, capitalists' drive to expend surplus capital in profitable ventures also took them to parts of the globe where they had little, if any, control over the territory.

Revisionist historians, most eminently William Appleman Williams, have made a parallel argument, namely that the shift from European-centered power in the nineteenth century to an "American Century" brought a world in which political and military control of territories was no longer the *sine qua non* of empire. While there is a lot of truth to this argument, it eventually falls on the wrong side of geography. 1898 was not quite such a sharp break: European empires had their own experiments with free market imperialism—most notably Britain in the 1850s—that distanced themselves from direct territorial possession. And they also joined the experiment of global economic domination without colonies, especially after World War II. By corollary, as the wars in Afghanistan and Iraq suggest, not to mention Vietnam, geopolitical power up to and including military and political occupation remains a plausible option for modern imperialism. While the recognition of revisionists that the critical role of territory has changed since the end of the twentieth century is astute, their eschewal of territorial questions entirely expresses more than it contests the "lost geography," and it misses the new twentieth century articulation of geography and economics which reverses the priority of geo-economics and geopolitics in the calculation of imperial interest.

More recently and from a different direction, Antonio Negri and Michael Hardt have argued that the new empire of twenty-first century capitalism is "deterritorialized," post-imperial, and certainly not identifiable with the United States in any meaningful sense.[12] Without knowing it, they have recapitulated the 1904 notion of Sir Halford Mackinder that "an Empire of the World" was just around the corner.[13] Geographer, liberal, member of parliament, and staunch defender of the British Empire, Mackinder presumed that empire would have a British rather than American accent, but Hardt and Negri ought to have had no such blind spot. They capture astutely the deterritorializing impulse of globalization, but are entirely blind to the converse reterritorialization that globalization also brings. Even before 9/11 and the Afghan and Iraq wars, before the hardening of US national borders, it should have been obvious that whatever the power of the global, imperialism—however much it now operates through geo-economic more than geopolitical calculation—never relinquishes territorial definition. Power is never deterritorialized; it is always specific to particular places. Reterritorialization counters deterritorialization at every turn.

American globalism from Teddy Roosevelt and Woodrow Wilson to Bill Clinton and George W. Bush is the consummate expression of the liberalism that founded the United States. Territorially specific, it aspires endlessly but never successfully not to be. Globalization is the capitalist expression of eighteenth century liberal universalism—"Liberty," says George Bush, "is universal." It was a contested liberalism to be sure, never as pure as the scholarly doctrines that came to be claimed for it, nor fixed in stone since the eighteenth century. Rather it took many forms, including the McCarthyism—and responses to it—that drove Louis Hartz to question the dogmatism of this most undogmatic political tradition. It was sufficiently victorious that by the twentieth century, the central antagonism in American politics—that between conservatives and liberals—actually represented an internal squabble within a triumphant liberalism. Twenty-first century American globalism, whether by neoliberal or neoconservative means, is its most ambitious fruit.

3

A GLOBAL MONROE

DOCTRINE?

It is curious to see America, the United States, looking on herself, first, as a sort of natural peacemaker, then as a moral protagonist in this terrible time. No nation is less fitted for this role. For two or more centuries America has marched proudly in the van of human hatred,– making bonfires of human flesh and laughing at them hideously, and making the insulting of millions more than a matter of dislike, – rather a great religion, a world war-cry....

W. E. B. Du Bois, 1919

"Americanism" brings McCarthyism together with Wilson.

Louis Hartz, 1955

On November 19, 2003, on a highly publicized trip to Britain aimed at propping up his main wartime ally, George W. Bush spoke in Whitehall before parliamentarians and foreign affairs leaders, and he prominently invoked the name of that great liberal internationalist Woodrow Wilson. Wilson, eighty-five years earlier, was the last US president to stay at Buckingham Palace, Bush crowed, but otherwise, few paid much attention to the details of his speech. It was, after all, one of these inane, platitudinous deliveries that politicians make in which the good and mighty are praised while the bad are condemned as evil. Bush praised Wilson but bemoaned the fate of his cherished League of Nations: "The League of Nations, lacking both credibility and will, collapsed at the first challenge of the dictators. Free nations failed to recognize, much less confront, the aggressive evil in plain sight. And so the dictators went about their business ... bringing death to innocent people in this city and across the world, and filling the last century with violence and genocide." In this flurry of wishful thinking, Bush was not simply blaming the victim of a century ago—the League of Nations—but backhanding his own contemporary nemesis: the United Nations. He seemed to have conveniently forgotten that if the League lacked credibility and will it was in no small part because its major architect, the United States, refused to join, that American policy after 1919 was implicated in the rise of fascism in Italy, and that the unnamed dictators were excluded from the League at its birth.

If the details of Bush's speech went largely unheeded, the very fact of his reference to Wilson drew considerable astonishment on both sides of the Atlantic: Dubya and Wilson? Some thought that Bush was simply playing for effect: Wilson after all had taken London by storm with his 1918 address to Parliament. Others thought the reference to Wilson a cynical and rather pathetic grab for that predecessor's idealist mantle, grandstanding on the back of Wilson's heroic arrival on the SS *George Washington* as the self-ordained savior of Europe after World War I. Others simply dismissed the reference to Wilson as an opportunistic rhetorical flourish aimed at the morning's headlines. Almost everyone snickered at the extraordinary political disconnect between George W. Bush, warmonger of Iraq, and Woodrow Wilson, sadly failed champion of the League of Nations. Bush came to Britain to shore up a failing and unpopular Iraq war and to support Prime Minister Tony Blair, generally disparaged in Britain as "Bush's poodle," but judging by his reception, Bush was no Woodrow Wilson. The poodle's master was politely but coolly received, with very little of the obeisant applause that has come to punctuate every sentence of such addresses in the US, whereas Wilson received a standing ovation in Parliament. At first blush, then, Wilson does seem a curious historical horse for Bush to hitch his war chariot to, but incongruous as it might seem through the anomalous lenses of a twentieth-century American liberalism that judges the world along a crude axis of liberal versus conservative, a solid political tradition connects Bush to Wilson.

Idealism and Naïveté in Paris

Through the lens of twentieth-century American liberalism, which he more than anyone helped to fashion, Woodrow Wilson has come to epitomize one or both of the twinned emblematic faults of that liberalism. By some, generally more sympathetic critics and commentators, he is seen as unredeemably idealistic, a brave warrior for peace, a man whose convictions overruled even national self-interest for the greater global good. His "new diplomacy" was intended to take the high road away from the internecine territorial squabbles that dominated nineteenth-century geopolitical struggles up to and including World War I. "Open covenants of peace openly arrived at," was the opening requirement in Wilson's famous "Fourteen Points," issued in January 1918 as a precursor for peace talks: "mutual guarantees of political independence and territorial integrity to great and small nations alike," is how he concluded the Points. Supporters generally lament that Wilson's idealist internationalism—a global liberalism of the most beneficent pedigree—was thwarted by the ruthless leaders of European powers that for centuries had been at each others' throats over territory and resources and were not about to change for the sake of a Virginia-born Presbyterian professor-turned-President. Wilson's liberal globalism was the legitimate offspring of earlier and nastier doctrines of manifest destiny and it was mooted by a powerful nation that for the first time was making global claims. With Wilson's defeat, that globalism lost its first and best chance.

To more critical opponents, Wilson's idealism is less a cause for lament than for disdain. By this version, he was simply naive: out of his league with the major political figures of Europe when he sailed to the Paris Peace Conference in 1918, he was gulled by the adoration of the masses and very quickly pummeled by ruthless leaders whose grasp of the avarice of human nature easily trumped Wilson's wishful idealism. He gravely mistook the emotional response of the desperate populace, celebrating the end of a dreadful war and grasping for any straw of hope for the future, as a real commitment to a new diplomacy in which nations would for the first time treat each other as "brothers" in a common, peaceful cause. This was the attack leveled by many Republicans in the United States at the time, and one that came to stick. For them he brought back too little too late from Europe, and what he brought back did more damage than good to a republic that was not about to allow any other power the merest suggestion of influence over anything the sovereign United States decided to do (especially under the auspices of the Monroe Doctrine). Not only was he unable to plant his vapid idealism in anything approximating fertile soil; the idealism itself was dangerous.

Even more damaging was the attack from an unlikely quarter abroad which seemed to support the latter conservative assessment. The budding British economist, John Maynard Keynes, later to become the architect of welfare economics, had attended the Paris conference, left in disgust, and quickly published a tell-all bestseller, *The Economic Consequences of the Peace*. He flayed the Peace treaty and Wilson in particular. When the President sailed for Europe, Keynes recorded, "he enjoyed a prestige and a moral influence throughout the world unequaled in world history.... With what curiosity, anxiety and hope" did Europeans seek "a glimpse of the features and bearing of the man of destiny who, coming from the West, was to bring healing to the wounds of the ancient parent of his civilization and lay for us the foundations of the future." But it was a "Carthaginian peace," Keynes concluded, and Wilson's failed idealism was a major cause: the President, quite simply, was bamboozled. Intellectually and politically unprepared for the wiles of French premier Clemenceau and Britain's Lloyd George, he was reduced to "playing blind man's bluff in that party," becoming a tilting "Don Quixote" to the hard-nosed avarice of European power politics. He was fatally stubborn to compromise yet in the end he also betrayed his own idealism.[1]

This rejection of Wilson by Republicans on one side and Keynes on the other carried far more weight than the sympathetic laments of his defenders. Although now increasingly stale, the emergent language of realism and idealism set the pattern for assessments—pro and con—of Wilson in Paris. As Wilson chronicler Arthur Link has put it: "The Paris peace settlement reveals more than any other episode of the twentieth century the tension between the ideal and real in history."[2] But this language was more than simply an exceptional product of history—it helped to make history. It came to provide the liberal template on which twentieth-century US foreign policy was to be judged. It still organizes many histories and international relations treatments of foreign policy. Realists are generally the more conservative analysts, emphasizing the importance of territorial control, the necessity of naked military power and the willingness to use it; idealists believe in diplomacy, negotiation and the ability to create progressive outcomes by talking issues through and constantly searching for workable compromises. There are clear echoes of this heritage in the contemporary *frisson* between neoconservatives populating the Bush administration, such as those aligned with the Project for a New American Century, and neoliberals of the Clinton sort who have been much less combative, more multilateral, and arguably more effective in their efforts at global control.

But the crucial point is that defenders and detractors alike are Wilson's children: they take uncritically the old Presbyterian's own proclamations of idealism. Those judging Woodrow Wilson naive and those thinking him a tragically misguided idealist have bought and followed the same script: none disagree that Wilson was a liberal idealist. They may differ on the advisability and efficacy of that idealism but they do not question the idealism itself. Yet Keynes's attack in particular raises trenchant questions, and it is difficult not to feel a little sympathy for Wilson in wake of the Englishman's indictment. Keynes criticizes Wilson as hopelessly stubborn in defense of his ideals yet also lambasts him for betraying these same ideals—he becomes both victim and perpetrator of failure in Paris. The contradictoriness of this indictment is symptomatic not only of the struggle Wilson waged but of the liberalism of his detractors too, including Keynes.

At a personal level, Wilson did indeed prove himself at Paris to be both a tireless searcher for compromise and yet extraordinarily obdurate when he felt he had right behind him. Whether he was struggling with Italians and Yugoslavs over the fate of Fiume (today Rijeke in Croatia), splitting hairs and watersheds over the borders of a new Poland, nailing down the conditions for the League of Nations or the details of reparations demanded from Germany, Wilson typically cast broadly for plausible solutions and appropriate compromises, and he entertained multiple positions and arguments. Indeed in the early days of the conference he was frequently faulted by advisers and adversaries alike for being too vague. But when he came to a conclusion on any of these issues—for example, the need to provide Yugoslavia a port at the expense of aggressive Italian claims in the Adriatic or his insistence on protecting Monroe Doctrine privileges in the League covenant—he unfailingly buttressed his position with high-sounding statements on rights and justice and dug his heels in stubbornly. His predecessor, Theodore Roosevelt, was not the only Bull Moose of the era.

This points to something important. "Our only political party has two right wings," Gore Vidal once proposed with typically incisive wit, "one called Republican, the other Democratic." Though written in the present era, this sentiment applies retrospectively. Indeed the writer Gary Wills explicitly denies the conservative/liberal divide as it was applied to Wilson. Conservative opposition to Wilson from senate leader Henry Cabot Lodge, among others, did not arise so much from any significant differences between them, Wills suggests, but from conservatives' fury that Wilson had betrayed them by being "a member of the wrong party."[3] By the same token, while Teddy Roosevelt, ex-police chief of New York City, is generally cast as the macho nineteenth-century conservative to Wilson's modern internationalist liberalism, they shared a Progressive vision on most issues, from the breakup of capitalist trusts to the need for social reform. Whether in Mexico or Haiti, Woodrow Wilson was no less the interventionist than Roosevelt under cover of the Monroe Doctrine. Wilson does differ from his gruff predecessor in one important regard, however. He understood far more clearly than Roosevelt the limits to territorial settlements and the territorial resolution of diplomatic conflicts and struggles and the need for what might be seen as a "post-territorial" alternative. Nowhere was this clearer than in Paris.

Therefore the traditional bifurcated view of Wilson—that he was either an inveterate idealist or a failed naïf—is less an accurate reading of his approach than a self-projection of emerging

twentieth-century American liberal dogma. The opposition of realism and idealism expresses the central conceit of liberalism; it
provides less a liberal lens on the world than a liberal mirror that
projects back a very specific picture of itself. Wilson has become
the most polished and expansive mirror of this twentieth-century
liberalism, making him a potent icon in today's neoliberal times.
But he himself was simultaneously idealist *and* realist to the point
where these terms were inaccurate then and are no longer useful
now; he was a nationalist internationalist, neither naive nor a
dupe. Judged by the rhetoric of "peace on earth" and an "end to
all wars," of course Wilson failed, but the naïveté here may lie less
in Wilson and just as much with those liberals who thought a
capitalist world built on global competition could ever yield an
end to war and guarantee permanent peace.

The League of Nations and Self-Determination

If Wilson himself is to be believed, he went to war in 1917 because
he was already convinced that a different kind of world diplomacy—a new model of collective security—could be put in place
at war's end and that his authority to mold such an alternative de-
pended on US involvement. A League of Nations was not simply a
good idea for the world, according to Wilson; it was a vital idea
for the United States. Breaking a pattern of nineteenth-century
non-involvement in European wars, Wilson argued over and over
again that the United States now had no choice but to become a
global player: "We are participants, whether we would or not, in
the life of the world....We are partners with the rest. What affects

mankind is inevitably our affair as well as the affair of the nations of Europe and of Asia." When the pretext presented itself in April 1917, with escalating German attacks on US commercial freighters supplying Allied ports, the President got a solemn declaration of war from Congress. He duly placed the guilt on Germany, but he never wavered from his larger aim—a League of Nations.

There were economic as much as political reasons for war. Wilson's public rhetoric was high-minded enough for public consumption, but he had become convinced that US economic aspirations would prosper only with an Allied victory and would be severely threatened by a victorious German expansionism. This calculation loomed large in his march to war. He knowingly encouraged trans-Atlantic commercial traffic supplying Allies disproportionately over German military and civilian needs. "No one," wrote a later isolationist, "thought of asking whether private American citizens in pursuit of fat profits had a right to involve us in a war." Wilson too was retrospectively candid: "some nations went into the war against Germany" because they thought that other nations "would get the commercial advantage of them."[4] To have a share of the spoils the US would have to be involved, Wilson deduced, but the President's ambition for spoils was both different from and yet more total than any of his colleagues.

Prior to World War I, wars invariably ended with new dispositions of territory, peoples, and resources as the victors took their spoils. But the violence of national state-making was also a natural breeding ground for ambitions of international peace, and alternatives had long been sought for international bodies and collective global associations. William Penn sent ideas to Europe

from Pennsylvania; Rousseau proposed a representative international federalism responsive to the "general will;" and Immanuel
Kant's cosmopolitanism seemed to require some sort of "world
republic." The liberalism that spawned empire also offered a more
forgiving internationalism: Thomas Paine envisaged a "confeder-
ation of nations." Britain boasted a longstanding League of
Nations Society, and the horrors of the Great War lent a new ur-
gency. For many Americans, the US already provided a model of
internationalism, linking thirteen separately governed colonies
into a "United" States.[5] Socialist and labor organizations—some
opposed to war, some not—also supported a League of Nations.
Wilson adopted the idea enthusiastically and by 1918 became its
most voluble, visible, and heralded proponent. The idea of the
League became the final of his "Fourteen Points," the document
that guided his vision of postwar reconstruction.

At the Paris Peace Conference, the League was contentious
from the beginning. For Wilson, it was the holy grail of the peace,
but the initial French agenda for the conference placed consideration of the League at the end. A counterproposal by Wilson
placed it first, apparently in the hope that the structures and goals
of the League would be interwoven through the conference proceedings and that a quickly established League could iron out details left hanging by the peace conference itself. He wanted the
League discussions to be held at the highest levels while the
British and French favored the formation of a special commission, which they overloaded with representatives from the "small
powers." In an effort to keep the commission small, powerful, and
effective, and sensing the kinds of grievances that would surely
come to the table of such a group, Wilson began at Paris by

arguing against the inclusion of the "small powers" in the design of the League of Nations.[6] An inauspicious beginning, this was also a portent of what was to come.

Wilson insisted that the League's founding documents be called a covenant, deliberately referencing the radical, internationalist liberalism of his Scottish ancestors who in the seventeenth century had fought for civil liberties against the feudal lairds. Successive drafts of the covenant were considered almost from the start at Paris. The French seemed less amenable to a League but felt that if one was to exist it should have military muscle of the sort that could defend against German incursion. The British, under the Liberal Lloyd George, were more amenable but watchful of US ambitions. In successive drafts, the commission agreed on a one-nation-one-vote structure for the League but otherwise stacked the organization against the "small powers": it included an insistence on unanimous decision making. It excluded initial membership by Germany and the Soviet Union and, in order to absorb and stave off pressure from labor unions and socialists excited and emboldened by the Russian revolution and the uprisings of workers around Europe in 1919, it also established the International Labour Organization. Clemenceau, Lloyd George, and Wilson could be "sympathetic to the labor movement," suggests Margaret MacMillan, "at least when it steered clear of revolution."[7]

For his part, Wilson fought many details of the covenant, compromised much, but dug his heels in when it came to the Monroe Doctrine. The Monroe Doctrine was pivotal to the fate of the League back home, and the US delegation in Paris already knew that it was the touchstone of anger and annoyance among nationalists, isolationists, and Republicans. If independent US prerogative was not preserved, the League faced rejection, and the Monroe Doctrine lay at the heart of that threat. That doctrine gave the United States paternalistic power in Latin America—economic preference, political mastery, cultural sway, and "protective" military control—and while it was widely tolerated by many in the Latin American ruling classes who benefited from the power and profits it brought, it was widely resented among the popular classes. Europeans too generally resented the Monroe Doctrine as an unfair barrier to their own capital and influence, and in Paris they worked hard to exclude references to the Doctrine in the League covenant.

Having no illusion that a covenant without such protective provision could pass in the US, Wilson was defensive. Congress would not countenance any appearance that the League might countermand its own authority to declare war, mobilize an army, or lord it over Latin America for the purpose of exacting profit. He insisted on a clause making explicit that nothing in the League covenant overruled the Monroe Doctrine, and here stubborn pragmatism fused with effluvious idealism: "Is there to be withheld" from the United States, he pleaded, "the small gift of a few words which only state the fact that her policy for the past century has been devoted to the principles of liberty and independence which are to be consecrated in this document as a perpetual charter for all the world?" Americans who listened were moved, the French not amused, the British—"whatever." The delegate from Panama, a country only recently invented by the US, went along, but the Honduran delegate was incensed, to no avail.[8] Wilson got his clause.

For proponents of Wilson's idealism, his stance on the self-determination of nations presents some awkward problems. He came to Paris an unprecedented champion of self-determination for the so-called smaller peoples, and made no small rhetorical flourishes about the need to free people all over the globe from the shackles of external control. "All nations have a right to self-determination," he insisted over and over again. This only magnified his appeal to the common people, especially in Europe—if the American President felt such loyalty to our black, brown, and yellow brothers, what must he feel for us? Yet this posture drew indignant sniffs from the rulers of the colonial powers where, from London to Tokyo, Paris to Sydney, Brussels to Rome, sights were set on the acquisition of territories relinquished by German defeat. In the Fourteen Points Wilson had been characteristically vague—he called for an "absolutely impartial adjustment of all colonial claims" whereby in all "questions of sovereignty, the interests of the populations concerned must have equal weight" with those of the colonizers. At Paris they had to define what this actually might mean, and the central mechanism, conceived in Wilson's wartime think tank, the Inquiry, was the notion of mandates. By this means Wilson succeeded technically in preventing whole swaths of Africa (German Southwest and East Africa, Togoland, and Cameroon), the Middle Eastern remnants of the Ottoman Empire, Chinese Shantung, New Guinea, and a range of Pacific islands from being subjected to direct European colonialism. But it was a shallow victory. In many places Allied recolonization was a military fait accompli. European powers were required to report on their mandates to the League of Nations, but in practice little changed except the language and uniform of the colonizers.

Wilson has been faulted—not least by Keynes—for giving up his idealism at Paris, and the issue of mandates is a case in point. But the accusation is too simple. He did mount a struggle, and it can always be said that the principle of self-determination ratified in Paris began a process of winkling subordinated territories loose from European colonial control even if there were other setbacks—a civil administration promised for Korea, for example, was never enabled under Japanese occupation. Still, whatever the gains, Wilson did quickly allow them to be watered down. The more trenchant question, going well beyond the question of ideals, therefore concerns the depth of Wilson's commitment in the first place. The whole rhetoric of self-determination provided a very popular rallying cry, but in practice he was far less a friend of the "smaller nations" than this might suggest.

In the first place, the status of Monroe Doctrine republics and territories were never seriously on the agenda at Paris, shielded from consideration by the mantle of US claims. Attempts by representatives of the "smaller nations" to bring their case to Wilson inevitably failed. A young Ho Chi Minh had made his way to Paris to plead the case against French colonialism. But his entreaties, made while supporting himself with a kitchen job at the Ritz, never even received a response. Instead, "Uncle Ho," as he came to be known, helped form the French Communist Party and took the bitter political lessons of Euro-American imperial arrogance back to Hanoi, where three decades later the French were expelled and another two decades after that the Americans went down to ignominious defeat. It seems almost gratuitous to suggest that a small gesture in Paris might have saved a lot of trouble later. Or there's the Irish Republican Army, fresh from the blood bath following the Easter uprising against British occupation, who were also contemptuously dismissed by Wilson. Even W. E. B. DuBois, an American citizen and prominent black leader, was unable to gain an audience with Wilson on behalf of African claims. Fobbed off on Wilson's right hand man, Edward (Colonel) House, DuBois turned his attention to working with Africans, similarly snubbed by the Conference, to found the Pan-African Congress. Curious indeed, as DuBois put it at the time, and with an eye to the history of indigenous genocide and African slavery, to see the United States looking on herself as a sort of "natural peacemaker" and "moral protagonist in this terrible time," when in fact that nation has consistently "marched proudly in the van of human hatred." Again, a lot of trouble could have been saved: Wilson should probably have taken the meeting.

One of the earliest schemes for international organization came from a certain French scholar, Émeric Crucé, who in 1623 thought a congress of ambassadors from different powers could help solve the problem of war. Among the political entities he included were Ethiopia, the Indies, Persia, and China.[9] Wilson's supposed liberal egalitarianism does not look so beneficent, when compared to its predecessor of three centuries, insofar as Wilson did his damndest at Paris to exclude Ethiopians, Indians, Chinese, those from the Middle East, even the Irish, and citizens of his own country.

"The Doctrine of the World"

His defenders exonerate Wilson by the doubtless truth that in a bad world one can do only so much. In order to get the League established, he certainly gave up a lot. There is no doubt that the French and British, the Italians, and the Japanese too were primarily concerned with territory, boundaries, and resources at Paris. In Europe alone 3,000 miles of new national boundaries were drawn and tens of millions of people found themselves with new national identities after the war. More adamant on some settlements than others—Poland and Fiume/Rijeke, for example—Wilson on various occasions assented to new territorial arrangements while figuratively holding his nose. By critics this is often seen as a sign of weakness, a failed idealism, but Wilson was nowhere as shallow or naïve as this suggests. That judgement itself is naïve and self-serving. Wilson's genius was to have figured out that the future of US power in the world was not dependent, as European power had been (and arguably as all other power in world history had been), on direct territorial control. It could, rather, be organized through the market. This is not to say that territorial control was never important—Wilson fought over territorial arrangements at Paris as hard as anyone, and in other contexts he sent his fare share of marines to Latin America—but he did perceive that the most central achievement in Paris did not concern any particular territory but rather the creation of a political system that would absorb territorial conflicts while allowing economic business to proceed as usual. This was the subtext to his popular slogan that he wanted to "make the world safe for democracy." Wilson's willingness to compromise on specific territorial agreements was less a sign of weakness, as adversaries assume, nor an unfortunate necessity, as apologists are inclined to argue, but a calculated decision that the greater good for the United States would be served by getting a League of Nations up and working. This makes the short life of a flawed League more tragic, not less, from a Wilsonian perspective.

But how did this transition—from a European-centered imperialism based fundamentally on territorial power to a Wilsonian world of economic and political power largely dislocated from immediate geographical possession—occur? A major conundrum facing the US ruling class in the 1890s centered on how to dispose profitably of the unprecedented surplus generated by the economy. "Our condition at home is forcing us to commercial expansion," averred railroad magnate Colonel Charles Denby. "Day-by-day production is exceeding home consumption" and so we "are after markets, the greatest markets in the world." Wilson's political affinities lay with these same progressive expansionists who saw the world as theirs for the taking, and he had not always been antagonistic to colonies and colonization as a solution to this economic dilemma. "Colonies must be obtained or planted," he averred in 1907, "in order that no useful corner of the world may be overlooked or left unused."[10] The debt to Locke's doctrine that profitable use justifies usurpation is unmistakable here, and these sentiments were not so different from those of British imperialists in their heyday. While he remained focused on the question of expansionism, Wilson's attention evolved and he quickly envisaged a more subtle economic expansionism. Campaigning for the presidency in 1912, he still acknowledged that "we must broaden our borders," but the effort now was to "make conquest of the markets of the world."[11] So why the shift from a territorial to a more "geo-economic" strategy for empire, from the geopolitics of colonial conquest to the conquest of world markets?

Put bluntly, the traditional strategy of geopolitical power and control was blocked for US capitalists. With the strongest economy in the world at the turn of the twentieth century but with the world map already painted British pink all over, blue for France, and a series of other colors for various European nations—the Netherlands, Belgium, Italy, Germany—there was little interstitial geography left for American territorial expansion. The taking of Cuba, Puerto Rico, and the Philippines in 1898—the crumbs of the collapsed Spanish empire—were woefully insufficient to absorb the surplus capital, and the prospect of battling existing European powers, especially Britain, for new territory was hardly enticing. Moreover, as US leaders sensed then and as they found out from Cuba to Vietnam and now Iraq, it was not just the colonizers they would have to fight but the aspirations of the local population as well. Expansionism would have to take a different route.

The route it took did not at all leave geography behind, as many have concluded, but it did reconfigure the relationship between geography, economics, and politics. Henceforth the primary means of "colonization" would be directly economic rather than territorial. Instead of controlling the flow of raw materials and finished products with all the expense of customs, factory legislation, a civil service, and a military presence across the globe (in addition to the capital investment itself), US capital would refocus on controlling the flow of productive and finance capital into and out of sectors and places that could remain technically independent—self-determining—but that would, by dint of US economic power, be controlled, for all intents and purposes, by US interests. The "Open Door Policy," which predated Wilson's administration and was aimed first and foremost at Asia, was a template for a more global ambition on behalf of American capital. This vision of US global interests was uppermost for Wilson in Paris. His triumphant arrival may have brought hope to Europe but it also brought a pragmatic economic globalism that made the League a much higher priority than any particular territorial settlement. The League, after all, was the place where territorial squabbles could be arbitrated while economic business as usual continued. And the US could be counted on to be the dominant competitor in the emerging global market. The difference between Wilson and the Europeans was now clear. He too was interested in borders, territory, and resources but whereas for the Europeans these were generally the end of negotiation, for Wilson they were more usually the means to the end. That end was a tranquil global political economy with the US as the most powerful player. The League for Wilson was a covenanter, Lockean America writ large: the assumption was that with member nations acting in their own self-interest and in competition among themselves, yet within an agreed international framework of rights, the greater global good would prevail. As historian William Appleman Williams has observed, the League "amounted to a direct and literal application of the principles of America's domestic liberalism to the world at large."[12]

So how are we to explain the apparent contradiction between Wilson's idealist proclamations and his actual treatment of the peoples whom he *said* ought to have self-determination? Put differently, wasn't the Monroe Doctrine a strange backstop from which a liberal devoted to "self-determination" would not budge? Wouldn't one have expected a liberal such as Wilson to have opposed the Monroe Doctrine's paternalism rather than to have used it as such a powerful weapon? Here we come back to the connection between liberalism and empire. It was not just the pragmatism in Wilson that mandated a defense of the Monroe Doctrine, although he certainly understood the hellfire that would erupt at home if the League covenant did not protect it. Rather, his defense of that doctrine was the act of a true believer. Geographically speaking, Wilson was as much a believer in the Monroe Doctrine as any of his opponents.

As he sailed to Paris, his ideals hardening in the harsh winter breezes of the Atlantic, Wilson wanted not simply a Monroe Doctrine of the geographical scope imagined in 1823 but a global Monroe Doctrine. As he had told the Senate, shortly after revealing his Fourteen Points, "I am proposing ... that the nations should with one accord adopt the doctrine of President Monroe as the doctrine of the world." These, he continued, "are American principles, American policies. We could stand for no others.... They are the principles of mankind and must prevail." Equal on paper, the nations of the world were manifestly unequal for Wilson and the subordinate nations were just that—subordinate. As he told audiences in 1919 while touring the country in support of the new world body, Americans should boldly "accept what is offered to us, the leadership of the world."[13]

It is difficult to find a more direct and honest statement of US global ambition, albeit one covered by the cloak of Wilsonian liberalism. But that is precisely the point. The Monroe Doctrine writ large was to be the successor to European imperialism. As the Honduran delegate at Paris understood, this was a dubious idea. Nor did the Europeans warm to the idea either. It was a rather haughty Keynes—not necessarily wrong nor disconnected from British imperial interests—who concluded of the Peace Conference: "Prudence required some measure of lip service to the 'ideals' of foolish Americans and hypocritical Englishmen; but it would be stupid to believe that there is much room in the world, as it really is, for such affairs as the League of Nations, or any sense in the principle of self-determination except as an ingenious formula for rearranging the balance of power in one's own interests." If Keynes himself was taken in by Wilson's thoroughly pragmatic albeit heartfelt idealism, he did at least discern that this idealism was aimed squarely at reorganizing the "the balance of power" in favor of US interests. The Europeans may control territory around the world, but Wilson wanted to control the discourse of global power in such a way that territorial acquisition was rendered secondary if not irrelevant. Wilson provides the classic and most accomplished case of what historian William Appleman Williams calls the "the imperialism of idealism."[14]

In Paris or on Capitol Hill, Wilson did not want scraps of territory, and those who chide him for compromising on this or that territorial settlement in 1919 not only underestimate his shrewdness but may themselves be naïve in disconnecting his stated "ideals" from the very real practical work they were mobilized to achieve. He knew that Paris would have to deal in the currency of territory: the world map, and especially the map of Europe, would have to be "fixed" before the bigger issue of global power could be tackled. It would have to be fixed in a double sense: it had to be corrected—old empires had to be dissolved (Ottoman, Hapsburg)—some states had to be reined in (Germany), and many new borders and states had to be made to align with existing ethnicities, social geographies, national differences, aspirations, and power politics. But the world map would have to be fixed in the second sense of being stabilized—the geography of the world would be made dependable so that diplomatic and geopolitical squabbles would be either resolved or else channeled into the procedural bureaucracy of the League of Nations. Paris was all about fixing the world's geography, and especially Europe's geography, in order to take it out of diplomatic contention in the future. Yet making borders and nation-states is obviously an inexact science, and Wilson well understood this. Over and over again he emphasized that whatever Paris did not get completely correct, the League could take up and fix: achieving the League of Nations was crucial to fixing the map of the world. In Wilson's hands, American globalism represented an Enlightenment universalism which would, in its wildest dreams, take the world beyond geography. It was literally utopian—aspatial.[15]

Wilson wanted the world, and he wanted it made in America. His espousal of a global Monroe Doctrine represents the apex of the first moment of global ambition for the United States—a world literally stamped in the image of the United States. International adventurism was one thing, global ambition another. For Wilson democracy followed the expansion of capital, and the United States, which found itself in the most advantageous position, had not just the right but the duty to "make the world safe for democracy." Bearing a distinct continuity with

earlier ideologies of Manifest Destiny and practices of continental conquest, Wilson's liberal internationalism was nonetheless
the first truly global vision of US power. Never before had such
a global Americanism come down from the clouds of metaphysical or religious fantasy and staked such a firm claim on the
world map.

Defeat

George Bush's evocation of Wilson in 2003 spoke volumes about
the long-term trajectory of US imperial interests. His oft-re-
peated claim that "liberty is universal" and the related resort to a
territorial rather than diplomatic strategy in the Middle East
smack fully of Wilson in theory as well as practice. By corollary,
the Wilsonian invocation—"we must broaden our borders"—
could well have been authored by the present-day White House
or Department of Homeland Security. The point for Wilson was
never that territorial calculations of a geopolitical sort were
somehow irrelevant in the new global order but rather that they
are displaced from center-stage, overtaken on a daily basis by
more geo-economic considerations. The expansion of the world
market had proceeded to such a point that in fewer and fewer
cases was it necessary to invade a country in order to access its
economic resources. Trade agreements, royalty systems for resource extraction, local taxation, bribes, bank loans, and myriad
other forms of economic "integration" were now sufficiently generalized that they could be called on to accomplish economic results that in the past required force. There would be exceptions of
course, but the downgrading of geopolitical calculation seemed

to follow directly from the making of a world economy increasingly replete with capital investment.

This argument can obviously be taken too far. It would be reductionist to assume that whereas European empires were territorial in nature, the American empire is "beyond geography"—that the power of territory is erased by the power of an aspatial global market. Britain in the 1850s had its romance with "free market imperialism," as did other colonial powers at different times, and for the United States the resort to military and geopolitical power—whether in Vietnam or Iraq—as well as territorial control was always available when deemed necessary. Wilson's genius was to glimpse that US global power could be exercised not exclusively but first and foremost through geo-economic more than geopolitical calculation.

Yet the Presbyterian Wilson did not inherit the world as he thought he might. He was defeated in the effort for a global Monroe doctrine—not so much by Europeans in Paris, although they were obviously instrumental, but by an unlikely combination of American nationalists and opposition movements both at home and around the world. The Versailles Treaty, it is well known, was defeated in the US Senate in the winter of 1919–1920 by a varied group of nationalists and isolationists, Republicans and a few Democrats, who all worried that membership in the League of Nations could commit the United States to future wars and conflicts that Congress may prefer to avoid. Wilson had calculated that his vague wording of some League provisions and his protection of the Monroe Doctrine would garner enough supporters, but his opponents wanted firmer guarantees. For Wilson, these escape clauses gutted the League and made its signatories little better than peripatetic volunteers rather than committed devotees. He dug his heals in against watering down any amendments, and the Treaty was rejected.

If the League was so good for US economic interests, why did it fail in the Senate? Why the retreat to nationalism rather than a brave grasp for the "leadership of the world" as Wilson promised? The usual answer is that, exhausted by the losses of war, Americans isolated themselves, at least from Europe, and this is true as far as it goes. After such a cataclysmic conflict, withdrawal behind national boundaries and assumptions surely brought considerable comfort. But it was a highly partial isolationism: in the 1920s and 1930s successive US administrations continued to intervene militarily in the Caribbean and Central America, operated an embargo against an unrecognized Soviet government, and meddled economically in East Asia. At the same time, economic expansion abroad by US corporations surged. In this respect at least, the period saw a return to the geopolitical calculus of the 1890s, and American leadership, having excoriated Wilson for his territorial compromises in Paris, was at least consistent in carrying that ideology forward. Idealists of a different sort, they devalued or rejected as dangerous to US self-interest any deployment of Americanism fused with global geo-economic leadership. It was one thing to invest in Europe in the 1920s, quite another to tie the US state to the establishment of political conditions there. The possibility glimpsed by Wilson was eclipsed, and the first phase of a US globalism was muted, captured, and circumscribed by a nationalism that failed to recognize the full extent of its own self-interest.

Opposition came from other quarters, too. Some of the very people who could have supported Wilson in 1919 were the targets of extraordinary postwar repression by his administration. Workers whose demands over wages and working conditions had been suppressed in the name of wartime national unity now erupted as their demands were rejected. They were harshly suppressed. The Army Reserve, upon orders from Wilson, responded violently in 1919 to a Boston police strike. And when Seattle experienced a general strike, a scared Wilson administration brutally crushed it. All over, demonstrating that the national borders were anything but impervious, workers responded to the initial success of the Russian Revolution and the socialist revolutions breaking out in Germany and Hungary. Workers and socialists spearheaded much of the anti-war sentiment in the US, and even in their consequent opposition to Wilson were overwhelmingly supportive of a League of Nations. In 1919, the President rewarded their support with billy clubs to the head, paddy wagon rides to jail, and summary deportation. The Palmer Raids—named after Wilson's Attorney General—illegally targeted unions, socialists, workers' organizations, and immigrants: essentially anyone deemed an enemy of the state. Wilson, it is rarely remembered, administered one of the most repressive episodes in US peacetime history.

The domestic uprisings of this period also responded to a racism that Wilson not only failed to combat but practiced. "Imagine that," he is said to have exclaimed, concerning the fact that Haiti was French-speaking: "Niggers speaking French." This may help to explain why, while happy to have blacks sign up for military duty, he refused to have them in units with white

Americans and had them put instead under French command. At home, he did nothing to reverse the anti-Asian discrimination of the early years of the century, especially in California, and throughout his two administrations he kept at bay not just W. E. B. Du Bois but black leaders in general. Thinking not unreasonably that a self-proclaimed liberal internationalist in the White House who had energetically canvassed their votes in 1912 might open up the violent apartheid strictures of post-Reconstruction America, black leaders were bitter about Wilson's disdainful rebuff. A massacre unfolded in East St. Louis in 1917 as black migrants from the south were brutally attacked by whites who feared for their jobs and wage rates, and Wilson effectively blamed the victims. As he argued vehemently for the noble cause of the League covenant (from which he had firmly excluded a Japanese-inspired clause advocating the equal treatment of different races), a spate of lynchings engulfed the South as black soldiers returning from Europe looked for jobs. In July 1919, unsupported rumors in Washington, D.C. had a white woman raped by a black man, and a race riot ensued: white civilians and servicemen marauded round town, savagely beating up any blacks they found. Wilson's derision toward anti-colonial struggles in Paris, his dispatch of troops to obstruct the Soviet revolution, his use of food aid to weaken a popular Hungarian communist insurrection, and his suppression of black political aspirations at home revealed the utter hypocrisy of any real commitment to self-determination.

Together, the nationalist retreat registered in the Senate and the broad opposition from below, both at home and abroad, defeated this first endeavor for a US-inspired globalism. The geography at

Paris would not be fixed even as Americans fixed themselves back inside their national borders, sealing those same borders from all but a trickle of immigration after 1923. They recoiled further as fascism in Europe seemed to replace the more progressive calculus of geo-economics with the old language of geopolitics. But this fix of US borders—social, economic, and cultural—was counterproductive and contradictory vis-à-vis US self-interest. If this became clear during the Depression, it was too late.

In a strange way, the nationalists may have been correct about one thing. What would a global Monroe Doctrine have looked like? How could the US have held and exerted such global economic control and at the same time have financed a military that was able to police not just a contiguous continent but the entire planet? If the nationalists were skeptical about such a project from a conservative point of view, the socialist opposition, largely supportive of a League, was horrified by the prospect of an American capitalism writ large. Ironically, the nationalist opposition, by defeating the League, managed to forestall exactly this latter prospect.

4

"A HALF LOAF":
BRETTON WOODS, THE
UN, AND THE SECOND
MOMENT OF US
AMBITION

> I was convinced we'd have a revolution in [the] US and I de-
> cided to be its leader and prevent it. I'm a rich man too and
> have run with your kind of people. I decided half a loaf was bet-
> ter than none—a half loaf for me and a half loaf for you and no
> revolution.
>
> **Franklin D. Roosevelt**[1]

The anti-globalization movement that burst onto the global
scene after the late 1990s—from Vancouver to Bangalore, Seattle
to Genoa, Quebec to Cancun—and blossomed into a global so-

cial justice and eventually an anti-war movement, took some very specific organizations as its central targets. The multifaceted movement targeted global and transnational trade and finance organizations and meetings of the world's capitalist elite, all of which were attempting a radical rewriting of the rules of global trade, investment, and finance in favor of wealthy nations and multinational corporations to the detriment of workers, poor countries, indigenous peoples, women, and the environment. As it exploded on the streets, the movement's targets quickly proliferated—the Davos forum for the global economic ruling class, continental free trade organizations, the G-8 leadership summits—but in the beginning the primary targets were quite specific: the World Trade Organization (WTO), the International Monetary Fund (IMF), and the World Bank. By the same token, when in 2002 and 2003 George W. Bush wanted global sanction for his invasion of Iraq, it was the refusal of the United Nations (UN) that attracted some of the most bilious diplomatic reaction from an American president in the post-cold war era. The previous administration, Bush conservatives believed, had subcontracted US foreign policy to the UN and it was now time to show who was boss.

Why are these organizations so suddenly at the center of global politics? What do they have in common? Apart from their parallel efforts to manage, regulate, and steer different aspects of the global political and social economy, as part of a larger globalization strategy these organizations were all conjured into existence during the same crucial moment of global history. The World Bank and IMF owe their origins to the 1944 Bretton Woods conference; the UN was consecrated at a 1945 conference in San

Francisco; and the WTO represents a 1995 renaming and institutional evolution of the General Agreement on Tariffs and Trade (GATT), which was born in 1947. What was and what is their purpose? What problems were they created to resolve? More importantly, how did these global organizations, spawned during a relatively short thirty-six month period at the close of World War II, become such powerful global players a half century later that they generated such extraordinary political passion?

The 1990s resurrection of these 1940s global organizations—including the US resort to the United Nations as the authority sanctioning the first war against Iraq in 1991—and the subsequent struggles over their global behavior can only be understood in the light of the events and struggles of the 1940s, a period in which US ruling elites again glimpsed for themselves the possibility of global ambition. The plethora of organizations invented at the end of World War II were global in scale but were disproportionately crafted in and by a multinational coalition devoted to US elites' interests. Their purpose was nothing less than a 1940s version of what we would now recognize as globalization. With the failure of Wilson's global Monroe Doctrine in their rearview mirrors, these organizations represented the crucial pillars of a globalism redux, albeit a globalism that was largely made in America. It was a different globalism than 1919, to be sure, but it was inconceivable without that earlier episode. It was also a globalism which, in retrospect, provided a crucial political bridge from Wilson's liberalism to the worldviews of Clinton and Bush.

1942 and All That

In an obscure and quite sappy 1942 movie called *American Empire*, a Civil War hero-turned-Texas boat captain plies the Sabine River and comes across cattle struggling to cross. The Sabine River marks the border between Louisiana (purchased by Jefferson from France in 1803) and Texas (marauded from Mexico in 1845). The Anglo-Saxon captain from the Texas side saves the cattle belonging to a Cajun cattleman and appropriates some of them as bounty for his efforts. The ensuing scene on the riverboat gives us the frontier in all its gendered splendor: a woman domesticates the "drunken hoodlums" who pass for crew, and the predictable romantic interest with the captain ensues. From his spoils—the cattle and the woman—the boat captain dreams about starting "a real American Empire" right there in Texas. As the story unfolds, it becomes a parable of good Anglo-Saxons aggressively acquiring cattle, wealth, and land versus lazy, suspicious, and sleazy French Louisianans, but it also morphs into the story of a patriarch-emperor of the prairies who rejects the common movement of cattle over his land and the coming of the railroad. He encloses his land with barbed wire, raises "No Trespassing" signs, and despite the entreaties of his neighboring cattlemen and the railroad company, refuses access across his plains. "We must get beef to all the country, North and South," he extols his son, quoting Abraham Lincoln, but this enclosure of his own land condemns his neighboring farmers to trek their cattle hundreds of extra miles to market, a diversion that drops their weight precipitously. Private property trumps collective social good.

Starring B-movie actors, *American Empire* (United Artists; directed by William McGann) presents the limiting dilemma of liberalism in surprising clarity: private property rights versus the common good, the individual versus the collectivity. That the movie is even called *American Empire* suggests not just the regional cattle politics of Texas in the 1860s and 1870s but the simultaneous angst and ambition of a stunned contemporary America wrestling with the shock of entry into World War II. The flawed capitalist hero defends his territorial rights against "ruling and trampling" by others—their cattle and their railways—convinced he is mounting a noble defense of rights. But his neighbors insist on their right of way, and in the range wars that ensue, both sides bear a massive cost. French cattlemen are massacred and the rancher loses rustled cattle and his son—trampled to death by stampeding cattle—his neighbors, and his wife, who deserts him as stubborn and impossible. The defense of individual rights, taken too far, can end in anti-social tyranny, the movie suggests, and a middle way must be found between isolationism and the prerogative of universal government. The barely concealed political morality play ends with a negotiated compromise: the Texas rancher allows the railway to traverse his land, for a price, and the neighboring landowners allow the rancher to keep his own private "American Empire" protected by barbed wire. Private property is preserved, the common good is advanced, and technological modernity is accommodated. Gee-shucks.

The year this movie came out Franklin Roosevelt was in the White House, embarking on a second world war. He had had to maneuver the US into war against an enduring isolationist sentiment with which he himself had dallied. By 1941 he was not only supplying Germany's enemies in Europe with war materiel but had instituted stringent economic embargos against Japan. The Japanese calculated, almost certainly correctly, that Roosevelt meant to enter the war, and provided his pretext in the attack on Pearl Harbor. Not unrelated, 1942 also witnessed an explosion of popular interest in geopolitics in the US. The fog of isolationism vanished in a gale of desperate curiosity about the machinations of the sudden new enemy, and Roosevelt exhorted the nation to follow the war in Europe, world atlas on their knees. It was also the year of an extraordinary revival of interest, after more than two decades, in Woodrow Wilson: from Washington to San Francisco organizations dusted off Wilson's heritage in the context of a new war. Franklin Roosevelt had served Wilson and was at the 1919 Paris Peace Conference. An erstwhile Republican who while a Harvard undergraduate had campaigned for the election of his cousin Theodore, the younger Roosevelt had become Assistant Secretary of the Navy in Wilson's Democratic administration, and had gone to Europe to oversee navy demobilization. No more than a spectator to the conference itself, but a student of history, politics and some geography, he was nonetheless drawn to where the action was. In a fortuitous turn of events after his brief sojourn in Paris, he found himself returning to New York on the *George Washington* with Wilson in February 1919, immediately following the conference's adoption of the Covenant of the League of Nations. He had previously considered the League "a beautiful dream" but too utopian. Yet was thrilled when Wilson, who generally kept himself aloof on such occasions, invited his Assistant Secretary of the Navy for a private discussion in the presidential cabin. There and in a later informal gathering onboard, Wilson extolled the virtues of the League, presented it as the only choice, and insisted that for the sake of the world and all it had just been through, the United States must embrace its possibilities and opportunities. It was a stirring appeal—the US must join the League "or it will break the heart of the world"—and Roosevelt, twenty-six years younger than the President, was hooked. When he returned he began giving passionate speeches on behalf of the League, was deeply disappointed by its Senate rejection, and when nominated as the Democratic Vice-Presidential candidate for the 1920 election, helped make a reconsideration of US membership the central campaign issue.[2]

For some, this history suggests that Roosevelt was infected by Wilson's idealism and carried his mantle forward from an early date. Notwithstanding his opportunistic waltz with isolationist sentiment in the early 1930s, how else are we to understand the priority he would come to accord the United Nations which surely represented, for Roosevelt, a kind of second chance at international organization? For others, the ample evidence of Roosevelt's hard-headed realism, which both predated and postdated his enthusiasm for the earlier League, belies any simple conclusion that Roosevelt was a Wilsonian reincarnated: the United Nations he envisaged was not at all the same animal as Wilson's League. Even with the Wilson revival in full swing, the President distanced himself and by 1943, according to historian Robert Divine, Roosevelt's internationalism involved a more unforgiving embrace of raw power. "By ruling out the possibility of a negotiated peace," in the new war, "Roosevelt clearly emerged as a realistic statesman who had repudiated Wilsonian idealism."[3]

The problem with this longstanding debate—Roosevelt as Wilsonian idealist versus realistic statesman—is that across the political spectrum, from right to left, among detractors and supporters alike, observers take as their political compass the liberal stereotype of Wilson as international idealist. It repeats the liberal conceit that judges Wilsonian idealism by its own self-mirroring criteria. Once we recognize the self-referentiality of Wilson's pragmatic idealism, as suggested in the last chapter, the picture of Roosevelt too evades such dichotomous treatment. Roosevelt's own emerging grasp of power during World War II and his clarifying vision of what he could (and wanted to) do with that power, represents a re-realization of global might, a reprise of American empire. In this sense he certainly followed Wilson closely and came to preside over a second moment of US global ambition. But this second moment differed in many respects from the first, and it did so in ways that have a direct bearing on the present predicament.

In 1919 everyone expected that questions of territory and boundaries would be of primary importance in postwar settlements, and they were right. The national mosaic of Europe, which had been emerging since the eighteenth century, was being shuffled into what participants eagerly hoped would be its final shape. Financial and economic questions were important, including the issue of reparations, as was the League, but in Paris geography was the stuff of global power. By the 1940s the question of boundaries and territories was distinctly secondary. There never was a peace conference that arbitrated new territorial settlements after World War II—these were simply laid down by a matrix of extant military geography, multilateral diplomacy, a swath of bilateral settlements, and eventually UN decree. By 1944 the primary issues revolved around trade and finances and the making of a new global political infrastructure to take over from the failed League. Accordingly, the big conferences at the end of WW II came in 1944 (before war was even finished) at Bretton Woods, where the postwar global financial structure was outlined, and the following year in San Francisco, where the UN was consecrated. Both sets of institutions—financial and diplomatic—were intended by their framers as catalysts and conduits of what we would now call globalization.

Another difference marks the 1940s compared with 1919. However much Roosevelt ran his own foreign policy, famously taking or not taking the advice of his cabinet and confidants, he was nonetheless surrounded by a much denser network of advisors and bureaucrats. The term "think tank" was coined in the 1930s as Roosevelt erected his New Deal, and with the advent of World War II he created a similar bureaucracy to handle foreign policy and postwar reconstruction plans, most notably by inducting the independent Council of Foreign Relations into the State Department (before the US war was even begun). The story of the second moment of US globalism—an American Empire right here in the US—therefore involves a much broader range of actors and struggles than in 1919, when Wilson's administration had very little—if any—foreign policy infrastructure to depend on.

Bretton Woods and the Internationalization of Finance Capital

The global economy of the 1930s lay in ruins following the 1929 Wall Street crash and the subsequent generalization of economic crisis throughout the world. A deep financial crisis in 1931 brought the collapse of international capital markets, the abandonment of the international gold standard, and a widespread retreat by national economies behind a spectrum of defensive monetary controls. The years prior to World War I had witnessed an extraordinary intensification of international capital movements, and with it the meteoric rise of the power of finance capital, that would not be equaled for nearly a hundred years. The world financial markets then were dominated by private bankers based in London and New York, including for example the House of Morgan, which landed immense profits by lending capital to European powers on both sides of the war. But all that changed in the 1930s. Private bankers' attempts to avert crisis, most notably the 1930 creation of the Bank for International Settlements, failed miserably, and the coming decade ushered in significant state controls on capital mobility.

After his 1933 inauguration, having bowed before the isolationist authority of publisher William Randolph Hearst and distanced himself from Wilson and his League, Franklin Roosevelt quickly established tightened financial controls for the US economy. Among other things, he reined in the power of the bankers, enhanced the sway of the Treasury Department over international monetary policy, took the US off the gold standard (which he swatted away as an "old fetish" of "so-called international bankers") and sought to shrink tariffs as a spur to world trade.

These efforts intensified with the advent of war. In an effort to stave off a threatened German invasion, FDR traded fifty destroyers to Britain in return for military bases in Newfoundland, Bermuda and the Caribbean, and then used US financial strength to initiate a broad-based lend-lease program for the Allies that ultimately included the USSR. As Keynes quickly realized, the financial terms of the lend lease program drained Britain's export economy and currency reserves. The "Open Door Policy" of the first years of the twentieth century attempted to wedge the United States into "the China trade," dominated by the Europeans and Japanese, and Roosevelt now sought to globalize that strategy.

With no little hubris, postwar reconstruction planning began in Washington before the US was even in the war. Treasury Secretary Henry Morgenthau promised "a New Deal in international economics," and quickly appointed economist Harry Dexter White to spearhead the effort. The Roosevelt administration now simply assumed that the US would play a central role in reconstructing the global economy, but they also knew they would have to work with the British: the City of London, after all, remained the premier center of global finance. With iconic British economist John Maynard Keynes, White drafted successive proposals for the world's postwar financial system. Given the financial chaos of the 1930s, the problems they faced were severe and their solution would have to be ambitious. They sought the machinery to stabilize exchange rates between different currencies, eliminate fluctuations in the levels of international financial transactions, supply funds to prop up economies with balance of payments deficits, and provide a multibillion dollar fund for postwar reconstruction.[4] Along the way, they also declared the need to stabilize raw material prices, create the means for amelio-rating economic depressions, and for good measure raise living standards around the world. But how was capital movement to be controlled without also depriving economies of vital capital? And how could controls be instigated without also providing the means for economies to indulge in financial protectionism?

The context was complex. The British sought to maintain the dominance of the City of London in global finance markets while the Americans wanted to open up the "sterling zone" for US capi-tal investment. This latter strategy was mirrored in the State Department which, among other things, aimed at "shaking loose the colonies" of the European powers for US economic penetra-tion. Both the US and UK wanted to defend their national economies against the predations of erratic transnational capital and currency movements and the prospect of renewed depres-sion, and in particular to protect their fledgling welfare states which they believed had helped stave off more serious working class revolt. Along the lines of Morgenthau's promise and New Deal thinking more broadly, the Roosevelt administration wanted enhanced government control over capital movements as a means of stabilizing the international financial system in gen-eral and the position of the US economy within it. They were largely supported in this by the country's largest industrialists, who in the 1920s had embarked on a frenzied multinationaliza-tion of production and who, while suspicious of the national planning agenda followed by White and others, nonetheless felt vulnerable to unpredictable financial swings and dislocations. But the US ruling class was split along quite predictable lines: the Treasury Department, which had wrestled foreign economic policy away from its traditional home in the State Department during the early New Deal years, was more amenable to Keynesian planning than the purer Wilsonians at State. For the latter, the crucial issue was opening up markets for US products around the world. And the bankers, unlike the industrialists, yearned to regain the deregulated power they had once wielded over international financial flows and lobbied hard to minimize the controls established over capital movement. The government should instead stand aside, they argued, and allow *laissez-faire* liberalism to have its way in the money markets. If this seems like a harbinger of more recent arguments between social welfare supporters and free marketeers, the comparison is apt.

White immediately envisaged an International Stabilization Fund supplemented by a permanent and powerful international central bank, which would considerably usurp the power of nationally based bankers, but Keynes—now Lord Keynes—had his own plan. After some wrangling the White plan became the basis of discussion as both realized that Congress would never accept some of the provisions in the British proposal ceding financial prerogative to the international body. The outcome was a proposal which significantly diluted the power of the institutions proposed, made the bank secondary to the stabilization fund, but had the advantage of broad political acceptability.[5] Presented to the July 1944 United Nations Monetary and Financial Conference in Bretton Woods, New Hampshire, these proposals designed much of the financial architecture for the postwar period. The conference was attended by delegates from 44 nations, but it was the US and Britain that undoubtedly ran the show. The Soviet Union did protest the size of its annual dues for membership in this capitalist club, but otherwise the conference passed largely as planned and the International Monetary Fund (IMF) and the International Bank for Reconstruction and Development, better known today as the World Bank, came into being.

The full globalization of the "Open Door Policy" this was not. However much the State Department may have desired such a result, the thinking in the Treasury Department was different. The IMF was charged primarily with the regulation of exchange rates vis-à-vis a renewed gold standard and the provision of short-term loans for governments with balance-of-payment deficits. Member states payed annual dues to the IMF for which they received specific drawing rights on the bank, but voting rights were also calibrated according to a country's contribution to the fund, giving the US Treasury Department, which contributed nearly 30 percent of the Fund's total, effective control of the new organization. From its inception, writes one analyst, "the IMF bore the stamp of US Treasury preferences and perspectives."[6] The IMF did enjoy some power in the 1950s and 1960s, especially in the area of currency convertibility, but until the 1970s, its disciplinary power remained minimal or untapped. The World Bank was also subject to disproportionate US influence, although it too never lived up to its initial ambition. As a vehicle of postwar reconstruction, it was overshadowed by the Marshall Plan and eventually transformed itself into a development bank devoted more to the industrialization of the so-called Third World and investment in the social infrastructure of these economies.

The framers of Bretton Woods were unsuccessful in establishing the wide-ranging regulatory power at the global scale that White had initially aspired to. Instead, they created an international infrastructure that left financial and currency control largely in the hands of national governments. Even this level of international regulation was challenged by US bankers, especially after the death of Roosevelt, and a more reactionary US globalism emanating from the State Department gained the upper hand. If the apparatus of global financial control had to take a back seat to Washington's political pursuit of the cold war over the next three decades, Bretton Woods nonetheless did establish a postwar international system of monetary control and financial and currency exchange. Bretton Woods did not bring a complete deregulation of finance markets; rather, it put in place a global apparatus of financial regulation where none had existed previously. The building blocks of that system were undoubtedly the national economies themselves, and this provided the central limitation of the postwar international financial regime.

Even this basic level of global capitalist coordination was too much for some. While the USSR refused to join, Harry Dexter White, for his far-sightedness in the name of global capitalist stability, was hounded by Joe McCarthy, who seemed to have a particular knack for confusing capitalist-inspired liberal internationalism for communism. One might as well indict the communism of John Locke or Woodrow Wilson. As for White, having sold his soul on the bible of patriotism during a House Un-American Activities Committee grilling, he died, still accused, before McCarthy himself fell from grace.

Geographical Arithmetic and the United Nations

If the IMF and World Bank became targets of the anti-globalization movement as the globalization frenzy hit boiling point in the late 1990s, the United Nations became a target of already simmering vitriol from the Bush administration after September 11, 2001. Central to US administration anger was the refusal of the UN to sponsor US war aspirations against Iraq, at least until weapons inspections were complete. The Soviet Union and France both threatened to veto any UN endorsement of the American war, and they were joined by Germany. Almost since its inception, the UN has been a whipping boy of US international reaction: while liberals bemoan its weakness, conservatives despise its independence. Only when its policies mesh with those of the US—the first Iraq war fought by George Bush Sr., for instance—is the UN embraced. Quite why the US should expect the UN to be a tool of US foreign policy instead of an independent global body is perhaps the central conundrum here, and figuring it out requires an understanding of the origins of the UN. Little if any of this historical discussion emerged in 2003 as the Bush administration fulminated about the French veto on the Security Council, yet the history of the organization and the untold story of the French veto help explain US antipathy toward the UN.

While the Treasury Department was building the edifice of global postwar financial relations after 1942, the State Department tried to rebuild a diplomatic infrastructure that would stabilize the geopolitical and geo-economic dimensions of the postwar world. Even if competition dominated the relationship between these departments, their tasks were intimately linked in Roosevelt's postwar imagination. The administration knew that they would have to deal with Germany again, and as early as 1940 the State Department had begun working through plans for postwar reconstruction. Whatever its sins, Germany would have to be rebuilt as a vital bulwark against the USSR, the State Department concluded, and as a mainstay of reconstructed European capitalism. The State Department still controlled trade policy, and if an expansionist United States was to avoid renewed economic depression, it would have to find worldwide markets after the war. This implied the need to sever the ties binding colonies to the European powers and otherwise open up the economies of Asia, the Pacific, Latin America, and Africa. As Secretary of State Hull put it with specific reference to the Middle East, postwar planning should involve "the fullest possible participation of private business in such government transactions."[7] Different State Department committees pursued these various policies, but the jewel in the crown of this administration's postwar diplomatic planning was the United Nations.

Legend has it that the name "United Nations" came about in late 1941 when Roosevelt and Churchill met to draft the Atlantic Charter on a destroyer off the Quebec coast. The charter was not quite the Fourteen Points revamped, but it was a clarion call to a united allied approach to postwar reconstruction. Among other things, it called for "equal access" by all nations to the trade and raw materials required for global "economic prosperity." After a long day's deliberations, Churchill, enjoying a hot bath, a glass of brandy and a stogie, was rudely interrupted as an excited Roosevelt wheeled into the room and announced he had the name for the allied coalition: "the United Nations!" However apocryphal this story, and whatever the real origins of the name, it stuck, and eventually came to refer not just to the allied wartime coalition but to the diplomatic organization established in 1945.

Planning for the United Nations began in the State Department in 1942. Isolationism had taken its toll even in a department led by the old Wilsonian, Cordell Hull. At first, the "committee on international organization" in the State Department, comprising officials and advisors, was undecided on whether it should aim for merely regional power, in line with the Monroe Doctrine, or go for a truly global organization. The Council on Foreign Relations, whose members dominated the committee, had earlier conceived US power in terms of a "Grand Area," centered on the Western Hemisphere and East Asia—but excluding Europe—which they ceded to the European victors of the war. But such unambitious foibles soon evaporated. There "will no longer be need for spheres of influence," intoned Secretary Hull, whereby nations in "the unhappy past" defended their interests territorially. The future, in other words, would be global. The geographer and presidential advisor Isaiah Bowman, President of Johns Hopkins University, was charged to prepare a draft preamble for the fledgling UN, and for him it was simply obvious that such an organization should be modeled after the US Constitution. "Certain self-evident truths," Bowman began, are universal to all nations and peoples. Bowman's prose was far less memorable yet much more partisan, longwinded, and even racist than the framers', and while it was thankfully discarded in subsequent drafts it nonetheless established the point that in the minds of the American framers, the United Nations represented the foundations of American liberalism rewritten on a global parchment.[8] The self-aggrandizing confusion of national self in-terest and American globalism tainted the design of the UN from the start.

Convincing the British and the Soviets of the need for a global diplomatic parliament, as Roosevelt first conceived the United Nations, was not easy. Although he never said so publicly, FDR sensed that solving the problems of war may be the lesser task compared with establishing an institution that would absorb the impulse for future war before it occurred. By 1943 he did gain their assent, however, and the following year a preparatory con-ference was held at Dumbarton Oaks in Washington, D.C. to hash out the details. As with Bretton Woods, the US draft became the document of record. Unlike Bretton Woods a month earlier, though, things did not go so smoothly.

The conference involved a three-way discussion between the US, Britain, and the USSR. The Chinese were also invited, but in-sofar as the USSR refused to ally itself officially with China for fear that Japan would declare war against it, and with the nation's resources exhausted by fending off Germany to the west, the Chinese delegation had to wait until the "big three" concluded their business. As the conference opened in August 1944, Rome had been liberated and Paris was next; the Soviets, at the cost of millions of lives, had finally managed to throw off a horrendous siege of Leningrad and were beating German forces back through Poland. Having waited three years for relief from the punishment of German invasion and bombardment—the opening of the long-promised second front in Normandy in June 1944—the Soviets were in little mood to compromise. With their eyes on the prize of postwar diplomatic power and the structure of the global political economy, neither were Britain and the US.

Many minor details were resolved but two issues were paramount: the voting formula and membership criteria in the new organization. The State Department draft envisaged a general assembly comprising all national members of the UN and a smaller body with five permanent and six rotating members. This executive committee would hold the real power, and it marked a significant difference between Wilson's more magnanimous design for the League and Roosevelt's insistence that the "Great powers" act as the world's policemen. The question quickly arose whether this "Security Council" would work by majority vote, unanimity, or some other voting formula. The US had envisaged a veto for the permanent members of the Security Council, ensuring that the UN would act only with Council unanimity. With the League debacle and Congress always in view, they saw veto power as a defensive requirement for themselves. But after drafting this provision, the State Department and Roosevelt began to have second thoughts: such a powerful veto could also be used by other powers to block US goals in the UN. They were not alone of course, but the US wanted to have it both ways: they wanted the veto for their own protection but wanted to deny its use against them. Finding a language involved a lot of close legalistic parsing, but to no avail. As the US embarked on a diplomatic bob and weave, the USSR resorted to the original State Department insistence on a full veto for the big powers. Deadlocked, the conference set the issue aside.

The second issue was membership in the UN. The State Department never considered any alternative but that nation-states would be the constitutive members of the new international organization, and this assumption was never challenged. But what counted as a nation? Soviet delegation leader Andrei Gromyko early announced that he wanted full membership for all sixteen Soviet republics on the grounds that they pursued independent foreign policies. Britain and the US were aghast, fearful that word would leak of the Soviet demand and turn public support against the conference. The new US Secretary of State, Edward Stettinius, insisted that in the official conference minutes it be called "the X matter." This issue too was tabled for later.

"Later" came in San Francisco in April 1945. The founding UN conference was the closest the world saw to a postwar peace conference, but this was not a conference of maps and borders like Paris. Amidst the optimism of war's end, many forced themselves to believe it would herald nothing less than prolonged world peace. After all, "to maintain international peace and security" were the words carried forward from the Dumbarton Oaks conference to the UN charter. But the loose ends of the earlier conference quickly began to writhe on the table, and whatever the presumed liberal niceties of a new post-conflict world, negotiation in San Francisco was a hardscrabble affair. On the question of membership, the Soviets wanted to seat Poland, represented by resistance fighters who had remained in the country during Nazi occupation. The US, supported by the Latin American delegations, wanted Argentina—until recently a tacit ally of Nazi Germany—to be a charter member. The US resisted on Poland, demanding that pro-West "London Poles" be represented, and an angry Vyacheslav Molotov hissed that something was surely wrong if the nation over which so much of the war was sacrificed was excluded while pro-Nazi Argentina was allowed in. Many agreed, even in the US. Journalist Walter Lippman "saw Stettinius and Nelson Rockefeller marshal the twenty Latin American nations in one solid block" and steamroll an agreement through the UN. Stalin compromised. He accepted only two additional votes for the Ukraine and Byelorussia while Roosevelt extracted two extra votes of his own (never taken up) for Hawaii and Alaska.

The new organization's voting formula remained the most incendiary issue. The Soviets were pilloried around the capitalist world for their insistence on a blanket veto for permanent Security Council members. "Paranoid," was the accusation: why didn't they trust the beneficence of their fellow conferees? If there was paranoia in the proposal, however, it may have come as much from its originators in the US State Department where the veto was first proposed in defense of US prerogatives, especially the Monroe Doctrine. But that truth was never spoken, and Stalin refused to budge. The resulting anti-Soviet howls in the US press are what is most remembered about the founding conference of the United Nations, as the USSR was cast as the villain against world peace. But in truth, the vision of world peace proposed by the US was heavily slanted toward US global power. Indeed, struggles with the British—over colonial policy and economic access to the sterling zone, for example—were sidelined in this dress rehearsal for the cold war. Even Roosevelt's friend, Sumner Welles, previously Undersecretary of State, came to agree that Moscow was only using the same defensive logic as Washington: arrayed against the other capitalist nations of the Security Council, "Russia's veto is her only assurance that the United Nations will not endanger Russian security."[9]

The 1945 San Francisco Conference was a catfight. Roosevelt had died on its eve and the protagonists were unsure what to expect from a brassier, much less slick Truman. ("If we see that Germany is winning we should help Russia," Truman had suggested amidst the early Nazi onslaught, "and if Russia is winning we ought to help Germany and that way let them kill as many as possible."[10] Such violent heartlessness presumably did not endear him to the Russians.) The new President endorsed Roosevelt's notion of Great Power leadership as long as the US was indisputably the top cop, but he also played the geopolitical card which Roosevelt had kept well hidden. FDR's 1944-1945 meetings with Churchill and Stalin at Tehran and Yalta had yielded territorial agreements, especially about Eastern Europe, that provoked apoplexy among newspaper editorialists and cartoonists, and Truman too was scandalized. Chunks of territory and spheres of influence were claimed by the US, Britain, and the USSR—so much for getting beyond Cordell Hull's "unhappy past"—and despite all odds the Soviets had now routed the Germans back to Berlin. For Roosevelt, much like Wilson, the real prize was not territory here or there—Poland was peanuts—but a postwar organization that would regulate in the forseeable future the real kind of international negotiation that would prevent world war. Truman's liberalism was much more conservative.

Conservatives who rail against Roosevelt for ceding territory in Poland or elsewhere at the Yalta conference have for sixty years missed the point. Roosevelt was neither out-maneuvered nor naïve. Geography was not the question. For Roosevelt at Yalta, whether Poland came under Soviet or British or French control was quite secondary. And did American conservatives care so

much about Poland in any case? Mired in an outdated geopolitical calculation, obsessed to distraction about territory relinquished to Russian influence in eastern Europe (territory that
many would find hard to identify on a map), and just as obsessed
about Roosevelt's seeming acquiescence to communism, it was
less Poland they cared about than politics at home. Whether right
or wrong, Roosevelt's primary calculation, like Wilson's before
him, was about institution-building. The crucial question was the
establishment of the United Nations, which could arbitrate all
such struggles in the future. Without the United Nations, he felt,
nothing good would come out of the war.

In fact, the document that came to San Francisco as the basis of
the United Nations was, as US delegate and Republican Senator
Arthur Vandenberg put it, utterly "*conservative* from a nationalist
standpoint."[11] This was precisely the point. Unlike the League of
Nations, the United Nations was to have strong centralized power
vested in Roosevelt's "Four Policemen." The four were originally
three: the US, the USSR and Britain. And had Roosevelt left it
alone world history would have been quite different. But by 1943
Roosevelt was getting nervous that whatever the hatred between
the imperialist Churchill and the ruthless Uncle Joe Stalin, they
might on some issues collaborate against the interests of the new
world. At the Tehran summit at the end of 1943, Roosevelt proposed to Stalin and Churchill that China be admitted as one of
the permanent members of the UN Security Council. It was a
shrewd move. FDR counted on the Chinese as supplicants whose
support could be guaranteed in the Security Council—the unforeseen revolution was still six years in the future. But the British
and Soviets were annoyed. Churchill's best of British racism—he

called the Chinese "the pigtails" and bellowed at the idea of Britain and China as equals among "civilized nations"—led the opposition, but Stalin too had little interest in seeing global recognition granted to a reactionary power on the Soviet eastern flank. But Roosevelt had done his homework and prepared the way with a quintessentially liberal appeal on behalf of the world's "lesser" nations, the importance of global democracy, and the rights of the world's most populous nation. It played to liberals and free traders at home and made him look like a magnanimous chap abroad. He got his way and China became the fourth policeman.

Now Churchill got nervous. With the US and China taking half the permanent votes and vetoes on the planned body, Britain would find itself in the uncomfortable position of having to make an alliance with ungodly communists—not a good position for the British imperialist with a brandy and a stogie. Churchill knew that given the US design, permanent membership of the Security Council would mean everything. If FDR's China card had weakened Europe's hold on power, Churchill sensed that Britain alone could not control the new organization but Europe still could. Stalin be damned. As much as he also despised the French— Churchill was nothing if not egalitarian in his disapprobation— the British Prime Minister now proposed that France should be made a fifth member of the Security Council, veto and all.

It was the US turn to be shocked. France had been overrun in a matter of days by the Nazis and no one seemed to like the haughty French heir apparent, Charles de Gaulle, who had camped out in London while many French men and women gave their lives in the resistance. While the Soviet Union held the

Germans at bay for more than three years, a Vichy government collaborated with the enemy, and the USSR, along with the US, balked: why should France be rewarded for its acquiescence? In the face of UK insistence, however, they caved in. The process begun by Roosevelt's opportunistic inclusion of its China ally gave France a permanent seat, with veto, on the UN Security Council. But it wasn't over yet. Roosevelt got nervous afresh and thought he'd return one more time to the well. Didn't Latin America deserve a seat? What about Brazil? By this point the tawdry politics of America's geographical arithmetic was utterly transparent and the proposal was laughed off the table.

When the UN charter finally passed, the general assembly included the Ukraine and Byelorussia as well as a veto for the permanent members (now five) exactly as the State Department had first proposed. If Roosevelt was dead when the UN's geographical arithmetic was finally calculated, he was nonetheless the host of the party. The Soviets had always complained that they were outnumbered in San Francisco. Western nations, on the other hand, accused the USSR of special pleading, but this was a disingenuous response. The Soviets were not wrong to see themselves as the only alternative to a fraternity that had clear capitalist designs on the new postwar world. Their attempt to include sixteen republics among the members of the UN needs to be weighed against the fact that the British counted thirteen nominally sovereign nations—members of the British Commonwealth—in their corner, and the US, quite apart from China, counted twenty Latin American Republics as part of its Monroe Doctrine bloc. All of the major players, it seems, came with backup, and Stalin, who was certainly a vicious dictator, was no fool when it came to geographical arithmetic.

Nor was Roosevelt. Campaigning as Vice Presidential candidate in 1920 and supporting Wilson's League of Nations, he had done the geographical arithmetic before. Trying to assuage naysayers that the League might go against US interests, he acknowledged that realistically, the British controlled six Empire votes in the new organization, but that Americans should support the League anyway because they could count on Central and South America. "Their lot is our lot, and in the final analysis the US will have far more than six votes which will stick with us through thick and thin."[12] Twenty five years later, the numbers had certainly changed and the players too, but Roosevelt and his State Department were making precisely the same kinds of geoarithmetic calculations as they formulated and fought for the architecture of the UN in 1945.

Successes and Failures of the Global "American Lebensraum"

World War II has been characterized as the moment when the American Century came to life. Announcing the American Century, publisher Henry Luce argued in 1941 that since the United States already enjoyed economic and cultural hegemony, damn it, we might as well join the war formally and assert "our" power in the world. The assertion of international muscle in 1898 seemed for many Americans to confirm the US right and destiny to be a leader on the global stage, and that the world actually needed "us" to take up this power. Echoes from 1898 to Luce through to early twenty-first century justifications for US unilateralism are quite clear. The cusp of World War II was in fact a moment of quite explicit global assertion by the US. A year after Luce's proclamation, General George Strong launched the idea of a postwar "Pax Americana." This language was appropriated from a pre-existing but critical anti-imperialism current in 1930s Latin America, but Strong turned it on its head to proffer an affirmative prescription rather than pejorative description.

A more telling triumphalism in this second moment of US global ambition is less well known and preceded Strong's and Luce's proclamations. Roosevelt's advisor, Isaiah Bowman, steeped in the geographical debates of the period, was well acquainted with the German argument for "Lebensraum"—living space—that had helped launch the war. As an expanding and muscular state, argued the Nazis, Germany needed more "Lebensraum" than the territory ceded to it by the Versailles Treaty. As the Luftwaffe launched a punishing attack in May 1940 against British cities, Bowman spluttered that if Hitler wanted Lebensraum he would surely get it. Only this time it would be an *economic*—not a geopolitical—lebensraum, it would be *global*, and it would be *American*.[13] Bowman's "American Lebensraum" brilliantly captured the larger strategy of the Roosevelt administration, the more so because it recognized the geographical dimensions of US global ambition. Destiny involved geography, Bowman said, not simply historical assumption; empires involve spatial as much as temporal calculation.

It was a beautiful vision of US economic and political power applied to winning the war and at the same time negotiating a peace whereby, as George Orwell put it around the same time, all were equal but some—most noticeably the US—were more equal than others. This was the larger aspiration behind Bretton Woods and the UN. In the making of the financial and diplomatic architecture of postwar globalism, the most ambitious aspects of the vision were certainly diluted in the various diplomatic struggles of 1944–1945, as was the extent and depth originally envisaged for US power. The US by no means got all that it wanted. But the institutions that emerged bore the recognizable trademark of the Treasury and State Departments and Roosevelt's wider global vision. That they did not work exactly as conceived certainly owes something to the details of negotiation that spawned them but also to the swirl of interests and social conditions both inside and outside the US during the postwar world.

For perhaps a quarter century the Bretton Woods financial system worked more or less as its framers envisaged. Government treasuries and central banks supplanted private bankers as the arbiters of international financial exchange, and together they established a system of monetary regulation. It was an uneven system to be sure, and the depth of its global reach was always limited by the national basis of economic power, which was broadly enhanced rather than diminished by Bretton Woods. Different economies placed various restrictions on currency exchange; many currencies in poorer or eastern bloc countries were not even convertible or had limited regional convertibility; some economies lacked significant stock markets. Still, a new system of international exchange now existed where none had before. With its own currency ascendant and its multinational corporations increasingly dominant in economies around the world, the building of this global financial structure disproportionately advantaged the US economy.

It was otherwise with the United Nations. There the national basis of the new organization had far more deleterious results. The unseemly struggles by powerful nations over membership, the veto, and the makeup of the Security Council alerted member states around the world that whatever the idealist speeches about everlasting peace accompanying the UN's establishment, its daily working would involve bare-knuckle politics based on national self-interest. It was less a global institution than an *inter*national one. The US never reconciled itself to the fact that a world body framed and fashioned in the State Department might grow up to assert itself, exceeding direct US control. Successive US administrations hailed the UN as successful only when it sanctioned the kinds of policies the US demanded. The Korean War was a case in point. Fearing a communist insurgency in China—which came to fruition in 1949—and in Korea (decolonized from Japanese control in 1945), and with the Cold war building toward a white heat, the capitalist powers at the UN secured support for the Korean War at a time when the USSR, boycotting the Security Council for its refusal to recognize the new Chinese government, did not turn up to exercise its veto. When the UN's decisions did not go the American way, however, the US was excoriating in its criticism. This was especially true after the mid-1950s when the "non-aligned nations"—the vast majority of member states which supported neither the US nor the USSR—exerted their power as a bloc to obstruct US and other cold war initiatives. On other occasions the US was simply embarrassed. In 1948 the aging anti-racist intellectual and organizer, W. E. B. Du Bois, tried to have the UN censure the US for racial discrimination against blacks. Blocked by a US delegation that included Eleanor Roosevelt, Du Bois turned to the Soviets, who brought the resolution to the floor.

The perpetual question, revived again at the beginning of the twenty-first century—whether the UN is and has been a successful global diplomatic institution—therefore depends entirely on the criteria applied. In terms of the aspirations of its initial framers, namely the US State Department, it has clearly been a failure. It has quite simply failed to become the hidden "third hand" of US global policy. In terms of its democratic operation, it has probably succeeded precisely to the extent that it has managed to stave off attempts by the US and other permanent powers to force their will upon it. The penalty for this limited democracy has often been ineffectiveness, however, and nowhere is this clearer than in the Middle East. Efforts to rein in an expansionist Israel have systematically failed as the US, sometimes supported by Britain, has practiced "veto by rote" against any efforts to discipline the Israeli state or force the humane settlement of the Palestinian question, the latter being a nation dispossessed of territory and without even a vote in the UN.

The national basis of the UN was therefore not only its hope, insofar as all nationalities were to be represented in this global body, but also its failure. The nationalism of the powerful that erupted around the structuring of the United Nations both anticipated and helped precipitate a much broader nationalism that portended a wider failure of the second moment of US global ambition. As the British-US poker game over permanent membership displayed, the failure of the UN was not an unfortunate aftereffect but was endemic to the idealist liberalism that hatched the UN in the first place. Circumscribed in public diplomacy, the US turned to more underhanded methods to ensure that it would be the most equal among equals in this new liberal international-ism. Typifying this turn, they bugged the communications of forty three of the forty five delegations in San Francisco—hardly an auspicious precedent for an organization devoted to global fraternity.[14]

The cold war marks an extraordinary failure of US liberal for-eign policy. As Stalin surveyed the world in 1945 from the unpar-alleled wreckage caused since 1941, he saw himself encircled geopolitically by capitalist powers in Western and Southern Europe, Chiang-Kai-check's China to the east, and the independ-ent and mandated states of southwest Asia to the south. The his-tory of Russian expansionism gave these neighboring states enough to fear. But the Soviet Union, taunted in the West as paranoid, was not wrong either. Stalin's strategy was to create a protective territorial cordon in Western and Eastern Europe and to seek influence to the south. It was a defensive strategy based largely on territorial contiguity—an insistence on a set of friendly buffer states—and explicitly not a strategy of global so-cialist revolution. For better or worse Stalin had given up that ambition in the 1920s when he declared "socialism in one coun-try" as the operative policy. The USSR would certainly support workers', anti-colonialist, and peasant movements in the postwar world, but this was secondary to the defense of the USSR, and the price for support was usually international loyalty to de-clared Soviet interests. It takes little imagination to comprehend that with the US atomic bombing of Hiroshima and Nagasaki—

an event timed and aimed to minimize Soviet influence in the postwar Pacific—Stalin might feel that his regional territorial strategy was a little wanting.

As Truman surveyed the same world he saw something quite different. He was as committed as Roosevelt to a global Open Door Policy but a lot less subtle on the relationship between geopolitical and geo-economic power. He saw a USSR that was standing up to US global leadership—impudently, he thought— and felt it should be slapped down geopolitically. But beyond this defensiveness, he saw, as Roosevelt had, a world that needed to be winkled open for US global trade. The Marshall Plan would help deepen and expand US interests and influence in Europe; China was girded to US power; Manchuria and decolonized Korea would have to be protected against Soviet expansion; and the atomic bombing of Japan effectively eclipsed Soviet influence there. South and Southeast Asia were in turmoil following Japanese occupation but in the immediate future the French and British if not the Dutch colonies would be restored while other economies, such as Siam (Thailand), would be opened up. For opposite reasons, Latin America and Africa were never really on the global agenda in 1945, the former presumed a US preserve, and the latter almost entirely colonized and of dubious economic value in any case. Nonetheless, Truman's 1949 Point IV program aimed at the industrialization of economies throughout the "Third World" as a means of opening up opportunities for US capital. In the Middle East, Roosevelt had moved as early as 1944 to reverse his opposition to the establishment of a Jewish state in Palestine. It was in no way a principled response to the horrors of the Holocaust, but a cynical attempt to win Jewish votes at home in a tight upcoming election, and it had global consequences. Yet at the same time, to secure wartime oil supplies and wedge US oil interests into the region, lend-lease funds were used to seal a strategic friendship with Saudi Arabia. In a region whose oil had been dominated by the British, the American Aramco corporation was the first and primary beneficiary of this agreement. The high postwar profile of US corporations in the region was secured when Roosevelt, returning from Yalta in February 1945, entertained King Ibn Saud on his cruiser and promised no change in his (already changed) Palestine policy without consulting Arab leaders. Thus was established a juggling act which has characterized US policy in the Middle East ever since—between the need for oil on the one hand and a domestically inspired support for the Israeli state on the other.

The geography that stuck in Truman's craw was Stalin's buffer zone in Eastern Europe. The Tehran and Yalta summits put Greece in the British sphere of influence and Poland, Rumania, and Bulgaria in the USSR's. (China refused the "offer" of Indochina, a decision that Churchill scorned as a sign of their unambitious backwardness). Consolidating his position, Stalin would later exert increasing power, in consort with local communist governments, over Hungary and Czechoslovakia, while Yugoslavia was reunited under the popular anti-Nazi resistance leader, Tito. The US complained that the governments of these nations were never opened to democratic election and in particular to the influence of the other Allies and anti-communist forces. That Britain and the US had themselves initiated the practice of "liberator's prerogative," having earlier installed a capitalist government in Italy without Soviet consultation, was passed off as the natural result of liberation. In Greece, Truman worried about a rising popular insurgency against an unpopular and repressive government and the British inability to handle it, and in 1947 he claimed the right—indeed the necessity—to help "free peoples who are resisting attempted subjugation by armed minorities or by outside pressures."[15] Truman promptly applied his own "outside pressure"—financial, diplomatic, and military—to suppress the popular uprising. Irked by the lost freedoms of East European citizens, Truman was a devout global new dealer and wanted more than anything to open the world to US trade. Not for the last time were rights made to cover for lost profits in a region.

There is no automatic evolution from Roosevelt's resort to national self-interest in the design of postwar institutions and the territorial hardening of the cold war world map in the late 1940s, but short of considerable foresight and magnanimity on the part of an economically and militarily dominant postwar United States, it is difficult to see how the political and territorial logic of the growing cold war could have been averted. But magnanimity is not a major attribute of capitalist competition, and nationalism, patriotism and anti-communism hardened the borders of the so-called free world. This time, in contradistinction to 1919, the nationalism came more from within the liberal vision itself rather than from without. There was certainly an extreme right-wing opposition in the US that saw the UN as a vast communist conspiracy for global control (it still sees it that way), but the most damaging nationalism was spawned by Roosevelt's own political maneuvering in a blatant effort to stack the Security Council. This may well have represented the final ironic nail in the coffin of the very body he wanted to make live.

As at the denouement of the first moment of US globalism, it was not just the fundamental nationalism of their world aspirations after WW II that became the Achilles heel of US globalism. There was also powerful opposition from a number of quarters. When Roosevelt came to power in 1933 the economy was experiencing a new nadir in the roiling depression of the period, and only the new President's rapid establishment of jobs, public agencies, and welfare schemes deflected more intense worker militancy. The threat of revolt resurfaced again in 1937 and 1938, but with war the AFL and CIO both made no-strike pledges, and after the Soviet Union was invaded by Germany and Stalin joined the war, the Communist Party (CP) USA enthusiastically signed on, placing FDR and CP leader Earl Browder alongside Stalin and Lenin on their banners. Many wartime strikes broke out nonetheless as workers in key industries—steel, coal, auto, textiles—were frustrated by frozen or barely rising wages while corporate profits mushroomed from wartime production. Pent-up demand burst at war's end with 3 million workers, many of them returning veterans, striking in the first half of 1946. The threat of overt class struggle of 1930s proportions haunted the country, and intensified repression against workers mixed with co-optation. Truman opposed the Taft-Hartley Act of 1947, but it passed anyway. It codified and regulated the opportunities for collective bargaining, mooted in 1930s New Deal legislation such as the National Labor Relations Act, but at the same time provided the legal basis for US military intervention if strikes were deemed "against the national interest." The threat of communism at home and abroad was generally interwoven in the justifications for such legislation and interventions.

As in the earlier war, black draftees in World War II were compelled to fight in Europe, Asia and the Pacific for rights denied them at home. Riots had broken out during wartime about job segregation and police brutality—a large 1943 revolt in Harlem followed the shooting of a black soldier by a white policeman—but the tension grew as troops returning home were thrust back into the same Jim Crow worlds they had left behind—back of the bus, "Whites Only" at the drinking fountain, and only the most menial jobs. A series of revolts for jobs and civil and electoral rights quickly followed, and Truman's major concession was desegregating the army, which most had now left in any case.

Much more important a challenge than after World War I, anticolonization movements which had been bubbling throughout the war exploded after 1945. Dutch defeat early in the war left their island colonies in the "East Indies" vulnerable, and a national revolutionary movement forced independence for Indonesia. The powerful nationalist movements in the Asian subcontinent made it clear to the British that they had no alternative, and a hastily organized independence for India and Pakistan quickly followed. In China, the corrupt nationalist government, largely seen as a puppet for outside capitalist interests, was overthrown by Mao's communist movement. The US itself was confronted by communist insurgency in the Philippines and relinquished direct colonial control in 1946. In Africa the process was slower, but postwar strikes and national liberation movements there also challenged colonial power, bringing a wave of independence celebrations from the late 1950s onward. In Southeast Asia, the French put more effort into retaining their colonies but without success.

Ho Chi Minh had transformed the revolutionary anti-colonial movement in Vietnam into a resistance movement against the Japanese, and when the latter were expelled the movement borrowed language from the French and American revolutions of the eighteenth century to declare its own independence. Having endured wartime brutality and famine, a million people danced and sang through the streets of Hanoi. But the rejoicing was short-lived. The world powers conspired to re-impose French imperialism, and the US contributed weapons and financing against Vietnamese self-determination. When the French were finally forced out in 1954, a UN-sponsored peace agreement (also covering Laos and Cambodia) made a temporary division between a northern region occupied by the popular revolutionary forces and a US-dominated southern region, but the agreed-upon election set for 1956 was blocked by US refusal.

The anti-colonial movements of the postwar period were a mixed blessing for the US. Having colonies loosed from the shackles of European colonialism was seen as a gigantic step toward opening the way for US economic intervention, and this was certainly the intent and fervent hope of the wartime State Department. But where decolonization left space for widespread revolutionary and anti-imperial movements, US prospects were seriously threatened, and successive administrations used their power to keep every national domino in the US cold war camp. Even in their own backyard, the US struggled against the democratic nationalism of peoples who refused the American yoke. In a reprise of nineteenth century gunboat diplomacy, the same year that Vietnam was ominously divided, the US unseated Jacobo Arbenz, the legally elected President of Guatemala, whose central crime was that he wanted to nationalize the quarter million acres of Guatemalan territory worked by the US multinational, United Fruit. The regime installed by the US rescinded the nationalization, liberalized conditions for foreign investment, curtailed democracy, and severely repressed its opponents.

In 1945, Franklin Roosevelt wanted the world but he knew before he died that he would not get it all. At home he had been supported by many industrialists—a good number of them signing on as "dollar-a-year men"—yet many more among the ruling class detested his "liberal" policies. One day he was visited in the White House by "a rich man" and Roosevelt, anticipating an attack on his New Deal reforms, pre-empted his visitor: "You hate my guts," he opened, for bending to the demands of workers and the poor, don't you? The rich man admitted that was true, and FDR proceeded to explain why he had established the welfare state. "I was convinced we'd have a revolution" in the US "and I decided to be its leader and prevent it. I'm a rich man too," he continued, "and have run with your kind of people. I decided a half loaf was better than none—a half for me and a half for you and no revolution."[16]

An unprecedented admission of his domestic strategy, Roosevelt's logic applied equally to his foreign policy. He sensed that the US would never get the whole loaf, but in the fight to get it they may just get half the loaf. That is an apt summation of the results of the second moment of US global ambition. If the cold war was a majestic defeat for liberal internationalism, insofar as Eastern Europe, China and eventually Cuba, North Korea, Vietnam and other outposts absented themselves from the US-led capitalist bloc, it was nowhere as total a defeat as that experienced by Wilson. Conveniently confusing capitalism with free-dom and democracy, the US could still parade itself as the "leader of the free world"—hegemon of half a loaf—while expanding and deepening its economic sway over that world. Whatever else it meant, the cold war registered the bitterness of the US ruling class at not also having the other half of the loaf.

5

THE WHOLE LOAF?:
GLOBALIZATION

Globalization has altered the dynamics in the White House, as
well as between the White House and the Treasury.

George W. Bush

I don't want everything in the world. Where would I put it?

Steven Wright, Comedian

In 2001, the new Treasury Secretary Paul O' Neill worried that
the huge deficit being run up by the US economy, and especially
by the government, made pre-emptive war in Iraq a reckless
venture. Frustrated by O'Neill's caution, an irritated Vice
President Dick Cheney shot back: "Reagan proved deficits don't
matter."[1] When this quote surfaced a couple of years later even
conservatives raised their eyebrows, and not unreasonably so:

this was the antithesis of the anti-government fiscal conservatism that Bush and Cheney were supposed to represent. The guffaws in the press were only muffled by the largely nonpartisan despair felt about the sorry state of economic intelligence in the Bush administration. The event quickly resurrected the label George Bush Sr. had once applied to Reagan's economic doctrines: "voodoo economics."

And yet historically, Dick Cheney was not entirely wrong. At whatever costs, successive US administrations had run mounting deficits, peaking (until recently) with Reagan, who managed to boost the federal deficit from $9 billion in 1981 to $207 billion just two years later. Clinton may have successfully balanced the government's books, but that has turned out to be a momentary lapse from orthodoxy as unprecedented deficits, into which the younger Bush plunged the US government courtesy of war and tax cuts for the wealthy, are and will be the new old reality for years to come. In the past, such long term deficits would have been unthinkable. Not even Keynes, doyen of government spending, could have imagined or would have condoned such a record of deficit spending.

How have the US economy and the US government gotten away with such unprecedented deficits? Bush actually out-Reagan-ed Reagan with a record $374 billion government deficit in 2003 and an estimated $480 billion in 2004, with deficits above $300 billion slated annually till 2014. Even the Congressional Budget Office suggests that as a result of the tax and war policies of the Bush administration, the government is tied into an accumulated deficit of $1.9 trillion for the next decade.[2] So-called "tax-and-spend liberals" look unambitious by comparison. The short answer to how and why this could happen is globalization, but on its own that is a facile response that raises more questions than it solves. Globalization is the shorthand by which we describe a dense range of economic, social, political, and cultural shifts that began in the 1970s, shifts upon which a third moment of US global ambition has been built.

In the early years of the twenty-first century, the idea of globalization seems familiar to the point of becoming an eye-glazing cliché. Yet a quick perusal of the index of *The New York Times* reveals that "globalization" was virtually unknown until a single mention in 1981, and that it went unremarked again until 1984 (Figure 1). Thereafter its use soared, peaking with more than 600 references in the millennial year of 2000. Broadly conceived as the process by which capital erodes and minimizes the significance of national and local borders, opening the way for global markets, trade, and capital flows, globalization is often assumed to be the inevitable—even natural—outcome of a capitalism that has swept away all competitors and stilled the regulatory instincts of national states. These states are displaced, supposedly rendered obsolete by technological advances in transportation and electronic communications. Globalization represents the apex of democracy, we are told, as previously excluded parts of the planet are connected to the most powerful, "the playing field is leveled," and equal economic opportunity becomes a reality where separation and disconnection had once enforced poverty. A more political narrative points to the implosion of the Soviet Union and Eastern Europe and the new capitalism of China: the other half of the loaf, kept from US exploitation by the cold war, is suddenly on the butcher block. It is, as

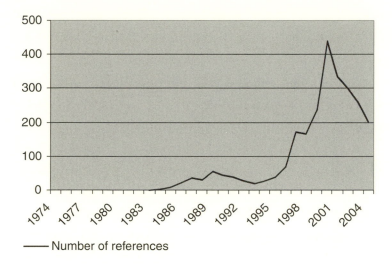

── Number of references

Figure 1 References to "globalization" in *The New York Times*, January 1, 1975–September 20, 2004.

Fukuyama famously put it from his vista on the philosophical shoulders of many before him, the "end of history." Globalization is inexorable, the logical conclusion of capitalism unleashed.

Quite literally utopian—the world is posited as aspatial, devoid of meaningful geographical differentiation (the end of geography as well as history)—this vision has dominated discussions of global change since the 1980s. The language of globalization plays out the contradiction between national specificity and universality that lays at the heart of US imperial ambition. It dovetails precisely with renewed aspirations of global power—a third moment of global ambition spearheaded by American capital. It replays the triumphalism of "the American Century" or the earlier "global Monroe doctrine," except that the Americanism of globalization is not explicitly referenced. At the same time, it is important to be clear that, however powerful US capital and the American state are in the construction of globalization, globalization is not the same as Americanization. Ruling classes around the world are heavily invested in globalization for their own interests, however much its central momentum may have an American accent.

To comprehend the rise of globalization, it is necessary to understand what the United States did with the "half loaf" it rescued for itself after 1945, what it gained, and what it still aspires to. This in turn has everything to do with the fate of the Bretton Woods agreement, its successes and failures, and the economic structures that supplanted it.

Global Finance: Bretton Woods and Beyond

The twenty-year period from the late 1940s to the late 1960s witnessed a level of economic expansion, both globally and in the United States, that has not been equaled since. As regards the United States, there were a number of reasons for this. First, a comprehensive series of labor accords diverted the threat that postwar class struggle might disrupt economic expansion. Sustained wage increases and bargaining rights were exchanged for no-strike pledges, as union leaderships themselves increasingly suppressed the most radical impulses of workers. Workers who would not be so easily controlled or co-opted were ruthlessly repressed, expelled from the unions as reds, or ghettoized in the inner city. Second, the provisions of the welfare state initiated by the New Deal came into full play, providing a minimal safety net for workers and their families. At the same time, such measures as the 1949 and 1954 Federal Housing Acts, the wide provision of subsidies to both the builders and consumers of the suburbs, and the federal highway program all boosted the domestic economy. Third, Marshall Plan reconstruction in Europe and rapidly expanding foreign direct investment in new plants and production further boosted the accumulation of capital (as did the intense re-armament that began with the Korean War in 1950). The Bretton Woods system of currency agreements and capital controls provided a basic stability in the financial system, especially as the European currencies again became widely convertible after 1958 and the Japanese yen after 1964. Overall, a certain integration pertained between financial, industrial, and social policies in the early postwar world.

The economic map of the world in this period was divided between a first world, with the US increasingly dominant, a second world centered in the USSR and China, and a third world of poorer countries. The latter comprised independent republics, newly decolonized states and states yet to decolonize, and they suffered, however unevenly, not so much a "lack" of development but an active underdevelopment at the hands of first world capitals. After the mid-1950s Bandung conference of "non-aligned nations," the latter exerted their power through the UN but still broadly lacked economic clout.

While US governmental and corporate leaders felt that they sat astride the world in this period, it was not to last. By the early 1960s, US-funded reconstruction of the Japanese and European (especially German) economies, from which US capital so benefited, ironically produced its own trenchant competition. It was a classic instance of uneven development. US industrial facilities, protected by geography and therefore unharmed during the war, were also protected by postwar tariffs but soon found themselves challenged by the cutting edge facilities and technologies of those reconstructing economies. Declining profit rates were matched by significant economic deficits in US trade, and these economic woes were exacerbated by the massive economic drain of the Vietnam War, which escalated after 1964. All of this had an effect on the financial system. The British pound was most vulnerable, but as the US Federal Reserve, in its own interests, supported the pound, the dollar too began to become vulnerable, and large quantities of gold were sold to sustain its value. The US deficit ballooned and with it the inflation rate, and the stability of international currency exchanges, which after Bretton Woods had been pegged to a rate of $35 per ounce of gold, was increasingly threatened. A vicious cycle intensified as the growing weakness of the dollar began to hamper the US ability to pursue the Vietnam War. As currencies faced increasingly severe pressure under the straightjacket of fixed exchange rates, it became clear that the IMF was no longer up to the task of currency stabilization. Its fund was too small, the US imbalance of exports and imports compromised the role of the dollar as a reserve currency, and the deutsche mark and yen were growing in power. Consequently, the US orchestrated a system of "special drawing rights" grafted onto the existing IMF arrangements.

Any respite was short-lived. The central issue was that currency speculation could lead to wild oscillations in international trade and the fortunes of national economies. The sterling crisis of 1967 forced a devaluation of the pound, which in turn led to a run on the dollar, and the US Treasury responded by announcing that it no longer felt obliged to restrict the sale price of its gold to the $35 figure. This had the effect of sending billions of dollars into European economies, effectively offloading onto them the repercussions of the US trade deficit. New US trade tariffs accentuated this effect, threatening a trade war with Europe. By 1971, with the situation increasingly untenable, a run on the dollar forced a reluctant re-valuation of European currencies, especially the deutsche mark. Richard Nixon convened an August weekend retreat at Camp David with his financial gurus, and the following week pulled the dollar entirely off the gold standard. Regulatory order gave way to chaos on the international monetary markets as currencies now floated relatively free of fixed or agreed exchange rates. The Bretton Woods system was destroyed, concluded one analyst, by the "struggle of the United States to increase its freedom of action in international monetary affairs. ... Step by step, the United States either broke the rules of the old order or forced other nations to break them."[3]

That this progressive rule breaking was always deemed necessary to prevent further damage to the international monetary system hardly mitigates its effects. The demise of the Bretton Woods system came neither by design nor by accident; it was conjunctural. The fixed exchange rates allowed little flexibility as different national economies progressed in different directions and allowed little room for adjustment to broader changes in the productive sector. It was eventually in the interests of the US—squeezed by deficits and pressure on the dollar, yet with unique free market power that enabled it to structure currency relations beyond the fixed Bretton Woods arrangements—to allow currencies to float rather than squander vast amounts of gold in defense of the dollar. If this was less a planned result than a matter of crisis management, it was nonetheless rued by the IMF. Even so, it solved few if any problems. The chaos in the international monetary world was not self-contained and was an expression more than a cause of broader and deeper contradictions. In early 1973, with the dollar under extreme pressure, money markets were closed for two weeks. In the face of declining profit rates and a rapidly shrinking industrial sector, the British economy also plunged into a crisis marked both by overproduction and a new run on the pound. The new Labour government that had inherited the crisis was abandoned in the international money markets, not least by British financial capital—the City of London—itself. By 1974, despite stringent wage controls, businesses were going bankrupt, unemployment soared, and workers struck against the disproportionate offloading of the costs of crisis onto them. Memories of imperial grandeur were wistful indeed as the UK government, in a stunning move, mandated a three-day work week. Even more humiliating, by 1976 the Bank for International Settlements and the IMF had to bail out the UK economy with multi-billion dollar loans. By this stage, the infusion of cash was no longer sufficient to stabilize the currency, and the loans simultaneously stipulated stringent austerity measures, including spending and wage cuts.

1973 was a crucial year for in the globalization of finance. Four developments are especially important. First, the world's major economies, including the United States, were all delving into a more or less interconnected economic depression that signaled the end of the historic postwar boom. Second and related, US trade deficits, which had averaged an annual level of $1.8 billion during the 1960s, now exploded to $11 billion by 1972, and as a result billions of US dollars poured into the world financial markets, especially in Europe. These funds represented early deposits into an emerging market, centered in London, which permitted dollar-denominated financial exchanges in non-dollar currency markets. Free from local state regulation, it blossomed into the bustling Eurodollar market of the 1970s which, by one estimate, amounted to 10 percent of the US money supply.[4] Crises in the financial and productive spheres were exacerbated by a third event, the OPEC oil embargo. Oil prices rose by a factor of almost ten; the embargo broke the monopoly power of western oil corporations, which nonetheless profited handsomely from the price hike; and the real losers were first the world poor who could no longer afford cooking fuel and second the governments of Europe, Japan, and North America which, short of invading the Middle East, appeared impotent in the task of providing their citizens with cheap oil. Denominated in dollars, the spectacular increase in oil revenues had to be recycled somewhere. The US rejected the IMF, and even as the New York City government went bankrupt in 1975, the private banks of Wall Street became the global center of petrodollar reinvestment. Recycled around the world, this capital expanded the Eurodollar market but just as importantly funded increased debt in Asia and Latin America. Many histories make the "oil shock" of 1973 the crux of epochal change in this period, but in doing so they erase the entire dynamic of economic and financial change that these events played into.

The fourth development of the period, and one which has been far more enduring, is the Asian industrial revolution. Since the

1960s a number of economies, most notably the so-called "tigers"—South Korea, Hong Kong, Taiwan, Singapore—had renounced import substitution strategies for export-based production. Squarely perceived in the West as part of the "Third World" in 1973, the "Asian tigers" were poised to catapult into the top ranks of national economies. They had in common not only cheap labor but strong state control over workers, capital flows, and the economy, and they were quickly joined by other economies in South and Southeast Asia—Thailand, Indonesia, Malaysia, Bangladesh—culminating with China's turn to capitalism after 1979 and India's "New Economy" of the 1990s. These economies too were fueled by recycling petrodollar funds.

1979 marked another crucial year. The leading economies had begun to stabilize somewhat after the nadir of 1973-1975 and the long stagnation that marked the decade, but only at the price of rising inflation. The situation was exacerbated as an Iranian oil workers' strike in late 1978 ousted the US-supported Shah of Iran and precipitated a new round of oil price rises. If these events initiated another global recession they also exacerbated inflation, which in 1980 peaked at a worldwide rate of 15.7 percent. The US dollar was especially weak and whatever the other economic signals, the Carter administration was determined to support it. The Federal Reserve chair, the cigar-stomping Paul Volcker, insisted that inflation was the central evil, and he hoisted interest rates to unforeseen levels in late 1979, in full knowledge that a deepened recession would result. They also intervened, albeit more cautiously, in currency markets in an effort to stabilize the plunge of the dollar vis-à-vis other major currencies, and as a result, international capital began to move into the US in unprecedented quantities. Japanese, German, and OPEC bankers particularly stepped in to help, and the price of the dollar surged. With a little help from its friends, the US had effectively been forced, without the intervention of the IMF, to follow a similar if shallower version of Britain's domestic austerity strategy. The intense Volcker recession of 1979–1982 was the price. Unlike its predecessor, the subsequent Reagan administration, guided by increasingly monetarist policies and blind faith in the free market, now renounced any effort to control the soaring dollar. The continuation of high interest rates not only attracted capital but restricted the demand for credit, and the "Third World debt crisis" ensued, felling the Mexican economy in 1982 and spreading throughout much of Latin America. Despite a domestic economic revival in the mid-1980s that followed the deepest recession since the 1930s, the US trade deficit exploded to $148 billion by 1986. Much like the Nixon administration but on a vastly extended scale, Reaganomics meant telling the world's other economies that the increasing price of the dollar was their problem. Sporadic intervention in the late 1980s cooled the dollar's rise before the 1987 stock market crash required rapid intervention in the opposite direction. The volatility of the monetary system was increasingly evident.

In effect, in the two decades since 1971, US and global currency policy had cycled through successive bouts of intervention and non-intervention, but non-interventionist "neoliberals" generally held the upper hand, even during the Carter years. On the cusp of the 1990s, the major economies of the world, cajoled by the US, settled on a comparatively stable system of target ranges within which currencies would exchange without overt interference.

Central banks always stood ready to intervene on behalf of a currency, either alone or increasingly in cooperation with others, but for the next decade currencies exchanged on a day-to-day basis with stripped-down regulatory control. By the late 1980s, then, out of the wreckage of Bretton Woods, a restructured, free market-centered, global currency market had been erected. It was sufficiently in place that after 1989 it could absorb, not without some problems (especially in Russia in 1997-1998), the new convertibility of East European currencies. The new financial system was dominated by the United States, a result which French economists Gérard Duménil and Dominique Lévy, with an eye back to a century earlier, call a "second financial hegemony."[5]

The global export of billions of US dollars in the 1960s, the renunciation of the gold standard in favor of floating exchange rates, the recycling of petrodollars, and the eventual establishment of a new currency system by the late 1980s all produced the need for a range of institutions to facilitate the new global currency and exchanges. Currency markets had to be established around the world in national economies that had previously restricted such flows. But a liberalization of currency markets could not be accomplished without a parallel restructuring of the broader financial markets to facilitate the expanded exchanges. The US had dropped many of its financial controls in 1974, Britain followed in 1979, and a flood of national economies followed in the 1980s, dropping controls on capital movement in and out of their national space. Britain's "Big Bang," allowing non-British securities firms to work in the City of London, came in 1986. Stock markets emerged where none or only secondary ones had previously existed, particularly in East Asia. While they initially provided a means of raising capital locally, especially in the light of momentarily high interest rates for US dollars, they quickly also functioned to wash wads of capital toward the US, effectively covering the ever-expanding debt of that economy. Given these and related changes, it was natural perhaps, especially when seen from the vantage point of the financiers themselves, that the process of globalization in the 1980s would be associated above all with the financial sector where so much of the old regulatory system was dismantled and swept away.

But shifts in the global financial system were only one thread of the so-called globalization process. And a good argument can be made that while the sweeping financial deregulation—a question of political economic policy—certainly represented a new regime for financial capital associated with the rise of neoliberalism, this should not be mistaken for globalization *per se*.[6] By its name, globalization connotes the geographical generalization of certain economic, social, political and cultural tenets and practices, and a fair case is often made that "globalization" is simply the latest stage of a much earlier global project, namely capitalism. That such financial practices were, at the end of the twentieth century, deregulatory and neoliberal in character is profoundly important, but they are hardly the only financial or social ideas and practices that have been or could be globalized. Bretton Woods had already accomplished a de facto financial globalization, albeit one that was quite highly regulated and incomplete insofar as the USSR never did sign up. Even more to the point, the financial globalization and economic integration between nations that pertained between the 1880s and 1914 looks extraordinarily similar to that of the post-1980s. As regards trade, there is nothing

new in the globalization of this sphere either—classical economists from Smith to Marx long ago recognized the vibrancy of
the world market. If post-1970s globalization does represent
anything new, therefore, it may be that we have to look outside
the financial and commercial spheres to find the source of this
world historical newness.

Global Production

The conceit of a "post-industrial society," promulgated in the
1970s by sociologist Daniel Bell among others, could only make
sense from inside the cultural bubble of suburban consumerist
America.[7] It certainly resonated with the wave of deindustrialization that hit western manufacturing regions in the 1960s and
1970s, but in predicting a service society beyond the need to produce, it not only failed to put that experience into historical perspective by refusing to see the significance of earlier cycles of
industrial decline and re-expansion. It also narrowly fetishized
industrial production, treating services as outside the productive
economy, and it failed to put the contemporary experience into
geographical perspective. The post-industrial thesis was dramatically blind to the world beyond the western suburban bubble.
Even as the epitaph for industry was being written, an industrial
revolution that made the European or American industrial revolutions look minor was sweeping Asia.

   Enhanced globalization in the financial sector after the 1960s,
therefore, did not imply an end to industry; rather it was
matched by a globalization of production itself. This had several

dimensions. In the first place, the geography of production was dramatically restructured. Spurred by low wage rates, a good proportion of modern equipment, and global export strategies, producers in so-called "less developed countries" expanded rapidly in the 1960s, especially in East Asia, but eventually throughout Asia and Latin America. This coincided with more than two decades of declining profit rates in the world's largest economies: in the United States, for example, the crisis of 1969–1970 was marked by a precipitous decline in profitability of nearly 30 percent. European growth reversed in the 1970s, and even the Japanese economy cooled significantly. Yet East Asia boomed. By 1990, the four "tiger" economies accounted for 6.4 percent of world manufacturing exports (up from 1.2 percent in 1965) while non-OPEC Asia (excluding Japan) accounted for 13.1 percent, a greater proportion than even that of the United States. This figure rose to 16.4 percent in 1995.[8] As a result, by the early twenty-first century, five of the largest thirteen economies in the world are Asian or Latin American countries that in 1965 would have been called, unequivocally, "Third World": China (6th), Mexico (10th), India (11th), South Korea (12th), and Brazil (13th). The economies of the Netherlands, Australia, Russia, Belgium, and Sweden all rank lower.[9]

But uneven development in a geographical sense is only one dimension of globalization. The rise of what used to be called the "newly industrial countries"—a nomenclature almost as quaint now as "post-industrial"—was intricately interconnected with a restructuring of production itself. Until the 1970s, the traditional organization of multinational manufacturing corporations involved a headquarters located in the country of origin and a

proliferation of branch plants and wholly-owned subsidiary operations in national economies around the world. Often geographically clustered in industrial regions, these plants produced
either for the domestic economy or for export to other national
economies, either in the region of production or back to the
headquarter nation. At the same time, smaller national capitals
also produced for the local economy and for export. This globalized Fordist system—named for the innovative organization of
the Ford Motor Company's production and the broader socio-
economic systems it helped establish in the early twentieth century—sprouted in the 1920s with the burgeoning of
multinational branch plants abroad and came to dominate postwar industrial structure, but it began to be supplanted in the
1970s.

As economic geographers have now well documented, a new
global corporate organizational structure is increasingly in place.
This new structure is buttressed by the twin advantages of just-
in-time inventory systems, which avoid the cost of long-term raw
material inventories, and outsourcing, which undercuts the
power of labor by organizing multiple sources for parts and materials. These multiple sources are rarely large factories and nor
are they necessarily owned by the central corporate power,
Instead, they may constitute a network of quite small and decen-
tralized production locations, even homeworking. A classic example is the multibillion dollar corporation Nike, the maker of
sneakers, clothes and sportswear, which owns no manufacturing
facilities but contracts with a stable of 900 factories and 660,000
workers, mostly young women, in more than fifty countries.
Non-ownership provides the legal and ideological alibi for dan-

gerous labor conditions, derisory wages, and a powerful anti-unionism, and as such Nike has become the target of a huge anti-globalization campaign.

These new industrial structures are often attributed to techno-logical advances in transportation, telecommunications, and com-puters which have enhanced the speed and capability of communication, reduced its costs, and thereby profitably reduced the turnover time of capital. Such technological changes are in-deed central, but they are not separate from wider transforma-tions in the conditions of capital accumulation, especially the increased scale of production necessary to maintain profitability. In the Fordist era, that need was met by building larger and larger factories; today, it means larger and larger networks of subsidiary, often small, producers. The archetype of this new model came with the "world car" in the 1970s: similar models were assembled in factories around the world from a range of suppliers providing parts for multiple producers. The world car was provoked not simply by technological needs and possibilities, but by the expan-sion of the market scale such that nationally based plants were no longer feasible—they had to produce for markets larger than the national. A new car plant in Wales in the 1970s could no longer produce profitably simply for the British market but had to take Western Europe as its oyster. By corollary, the outsourcing of work also undercut union power insofar as strikes in one facility could be circumvented by reliance on others. The globalization of supply sources, in other words, was intricately interwoven with the glob-alization of markets. A computer purchased in Hong Kong, for ex-ample, may comprise components from factories in India, Thailand, China, Bangladesh, Japan, and the Philippines, and final assembly may be in Hong Kong or perhaps Taiwan. The same computer bought in Reykjavik may have components from many of the same places yet parts also from Europe, and may have been assembled in Scotland. The two commodities involve different if overlapping production networks but are indistinguishable, except perhaps for the country that appears on the "made in" label. As an indicator of how fully the production process has been integrated globally, by 1987, according to one report, 67 percent of US imports and 81 percent of exports represent trade *within* rather than between multinational corporations.[10]

Less scintillating by far than the intrigue of finance capital, the globalization of production may account for more of the novelty of globalization. More often than not it has been the leading edge of global expansion. Whereas commodity production prior to the 1970s was generally aimed at specific national markets, and was rooted in the networks comprising sub-national economic regions—the Ruhr, Midwest, Yorkshire—today production is rooted much more in smaller scale city-centered regions and is aimed at the global rather than national market.

The astonishing levels of global migration since the 1960s, involving all the world's continents (and paralleled only by the more regionally specific migrations during the prior period of financial globalization at the beginning of the twentieth century), are closely interconnected with the globalization of production insofar as this human mobility represents a spatial resorting of workers attracted and repelled by changing economic conditions. Whether we describe the migrants in terms of variable capital in classical economic terms or human capital in neoliberal terms, this migration is integral to the globalization of production. This is especially the case if we get beyond a certain fetishism that treats industry as the be-all and end-all of production and recognize that a whole range of producer, transportation, and related services properly belong as part of the productive economy.

The globalization of production is not divorced from transformations in the financial sphere—far from it. Insofar as corporations assemble products with inputs from multiple national economies, the ability to exchange funds across currency zones became imperative. The liberalization of the currency and financial structures therefore received a significant impetus from the globalization of production. The rapid expansion of stock markets in Asia, for example, had everything to do with providing a consumer symbolism that not only attracted local capital but gave multinational corporations an advertising "peg" in newspaper ads and street billboards in the burgeoning cities of the region. A Korean worker clocking into a General Motors plant was not only a target to buy a GM car but also to buy GM stock. The globalization of financial capital is more accomplished than that of production capital precisely because unlike the latter, the former can be moved in huge quantities electronically or on paper with very little effort. Factories and office buildings are fixed, by contrast, over significant periods of time. But the ease of movement and more accomplished global sway of financial capital does not necessarily translate into causal priority. Without the globalization of production and the deficits that have, in considerable consequence, marked the US economy since the 1970s, the impetus for liberalizing and globalizing the financial sector would have been significantly diminished.

The Ideology of Globalization: Neoliberalism

If the economic outlines of globalization emerged in response to specific crises and contradictions in the financial and productive economies, the result, while not entirely planned, was yet guided by a quite specific vision. The core of this vision represented a visceral reaction against Keynesian state attempts to manage the economy and society more broadly. Inspired by the Austrian anticommunists Friedrich Hayek and Karl Popper as well as by American free marketeers Walt Rostow and Chicago economist Milton Friedman (among others), this devout commitment to the free market as arbiter of social as well as economic good coexisted with the half-century dominance of Keynesianism and developed a certain intellectual presence, but it was marginal to state policymaking. For these free marketeers, state intervention did not help regulate the economy but hampered it, getting in the way of higher growth and the market's proper dominance of the wider social economy. The successive economic crises of the 1960s and 1970s and enduring stagflation changed all that, however, and the failure of Keynesian economic strategies to restore either growth or stability exposed a wider bankruptcy of postwar liberalism. In the battle between left and right to fill the resulting vacuum, the free marketeers were the undoubted winners. Defeated social democratic parties in Europe did occasionally give way to socialist alternatives, as in Italy in the late 1970s when the Italian Communist Party came close to power. But the IMF straightjacket on the British Labor Party and the Volcker recession after 1979 signaled what was to come. The ascent of Thatcher and Reagan—and in Germany, Kohl—cemented the victory of free-market economics over any alternatives. It was in the 1980s that this monetarist and free-market movement institutionalized itself as a full-blooded neoliberalism, and its global political ambition was forcefully unrolled. As much as they were named by their adversaries, they had long taken the name on themselves.

Neoliberalism, it quickly became apparent, was about much more than economic orthodoxy. Within the kernel of free market logic there lay a larger social rationale. Whether imposed by the IMF or World Bank, the US Treasury or national governments, whether in Chile 1973 or Britain 1979, Mexico or Indonesia in the 1990s, the combination of currency and financial decontrols, tax cuts for the wealthy and wage cuts for the poor, austerity programs and social welfare cuts, and the repression of peasants and workers had highly uneven effects. In the first place, from the end of the 1970s US income from foreign corporate profits began to dwarf domestic profits as US elites sucked in surplus value from the labor of others around the world, and sustained their ability to do so for the next quarter century. Within the US, postwar economic expansion managed by the Keynesian state had seen a mild but persistent diminution of the income gap between rich and poor, a thoroughly intended consequence, but every indicator of income and wealth shows that this trend also reversed at the end of the 1970s. This too was a thoroughly intended consequence of neoliberalism. Whatever technical and ideological shifts it implied, neoliberalism brought about a concerted and regressive class redistribution of wealth as the rich got richer and the poor poorer. However much camouflaged by economists' diagrams and equations and the homilies of conservative, social individualism, neoliberalism was also a quite direct strategy of class struggle. A weapon of reaction and revenge—revanchism—it was designed to take back for the ruling classes and their professional and managerial consorts the "losses" that twentieth-century "liberalism" had visited on them.

Global neoliberalism blossomed in the 1990s. Internationally it was marked by the post-cold war "Washington Consensus." The Washington Consensus bound the elites of the advanced capitalist world together in a broadly shared ideological vision equating capitalism with democracy, free markets with human rights. It also provided an alternative to the now-defunct postwar model of development for the "less developed countries," which not only advocated import substitution—economies were supposed to develop by building industries that supplied their own needs instead of relying on imported goods—but encouraged state management of "modernization." The Washington consensus instead saw "emerging markets," erasing the social dimensions of the places they referred to; they emphasized not only export-oriented growth but privatization, deregulation, free trade, and monetarism. As the IMF, World Bank, and (after being renamed in 1995) the World Trade Organization began to play a more dominant global role under the ideological sway and virtual control of the US Treasury Department, they too became organs of the Washington Consensus, enforcing the doctrines of neoliberalism through free trade statutes, the discipline of structural adjustment, and the strictures of financial stabilization programs. Liberalize, privatize, deregulate! These were the nostrums of the new orthodoxy.

"Free trade," Texas Republican Dick Armey once preached, may be the most important "human right." In the US, and to a lesser extent throughout the advanced capitalist world, with the wealth of the upper classes now so disproportionately dependent on remittances from the global economy and from the sweat of workers around the world, this elevation of free trade to the most human of human rights was not only a brazen apology for global looting, but it eloquently marks the victory of a neoliberal ideology in which market forces attain the stature of natural laws, and the habitual winners in the capitalist jackpot defend their piles of booty as the product of natural right. Locke and Adam Smith are back among us in body as well as soul. If the consequent dismissal of any truly human rights—such as the right to a home, food, work, and security—struck some as callous, it was barely remarked on. And while the United States was the epicenter of this global class struggle, it was not alone and nor was this entirely a national strategy. Neoliberalism galvanized the interests of ruling classes throughout the world, not just in North America, Europe, and Japan, but in economies around the globe, including those that have either gladly or regretfully signed on for aid from the IMF or World Bank.

The Fort Knox of global capitalism after the 1980s, the United States was where the neoliberal backlash against Keynesianism truly blossomed. The ideological assault may have gone public with Ronald Reagan, but the dismantling of social welfare was accomplished under Bill Clinton, whose 1996 "welfare reform" law completed the work of Reaganism in a way that the former actor never could have. In addition to ending aid for dependent children and drastically limiting benefits for the unemployed,

Clinton also introduced workfare, forcing welfare recipients to work for token wages far below the parsimonious minimum wage rates, while also abrogating their right to unionize.

"Neoliberalism" was a label that early proponents such as Hayek and Friedman bravely took upon themselves. They intended it to differentiate themselves from the "social" liberalism associated with Roosevelt's New Deal and the policies of the Keynesian state that they despised. Most saw them simply as conservative, according to the political ideologies of the American twentieth century—liberal was left, which they weren't, so they must be conservative. We have already seen the peculiar American source of this unique ideological alignment, the transformation of early twentieth-century liberalism, in the absence of social democracy, into an antidote to communism. The early neoliberals understood precisely this diversion taken by twentieth-century American liberalism, and in emphasizing not just some traditionalism but their orthodox roots in liberal economic theory, they sought nothing less than to reclaim liberalism from its hijacking by Keynes and the left. Adam Smith was an abiding benchmark, but other economic theorists and of course Locke (though rarely Hobbes) were also referenced. As the movement gained power in the 1980s, its opponents seized on this description and more, probably, than proponents themselves, helped to popularize "neoliberal" as an epithet. Neoliberalism *is* modern day conservatism, much as the eighteenth century liberal tradition has long since become conservative in its own right.

The third moment of US globalism is so far quite unlike its two predecessors and we should probably be thankful for that.

Each of the two previous moments was punctuated by horrendous global war costing tens of millions of lives. In neither case was the US directly implicated in the war's causes; rather a ruling elite used the opportunity of war begun elsewhere to advance their ambitions on the global stage. In the 1980s and 1990s, by contrast, the US ruling class used its global power to follow the ambition of Woodrow Wilson, and it assembled a class coalition around the world to put in place something that closely resembles his dream of a global "Monroe Doctrine." Or, as the older Bush put it, borrowing the language of Franklin Roosevelt, a new world order. The coming of this new moment of US globalism was not entirely peaceful—wars, invasions, and bombings came to Granada, Panama, Kosovo, Serbia, Bosnia, Sudan, Iraq, among others—but prior to 2001 its substance was geo-economic more than geopolitical. Global and multilateral agreements on trade, weapons reduction, currency transfers, the environment, a judiciary, finance, and accounting practices—all of these traced the leading edge of globalization and neoliberalism, but they also sketched the architecture of an extraordinary geo-economic world empire centered on the United States. At the turn of the twenty-first century the architects of US global power knew they would have to compromise to get their way, but they also knew quite clearly that they wanted the whole loaf and they could see it in the power of the dollar and the clauses and whereases of international agreements that worked to their advantage. Those who took over sought a more impatient route to US globalism, and against this optimistic background of the late 1990s, Cheney's anxious retort that "Reagan proved that deficits don't matter" already seemed defensive in the extreme.

He may have had short term historical truth—a quarter century of US economic skullduggery—on his side, but long term economic reality is sure to tell a different story.

6

GUANTÁNAMO
CONVENTIONS:
THE BANKRUPTCY OF
LIBERALISM

... the basic ethical problem of a liberal society [is] not the danger of the majority which has been its conscious fear but the danger of unanimity[:] irrational Lockeanism that is Americanism.

Louis Hartz, 1955

I have the authority to suspend Geneva [conventions] as between the US and Afghanistan....I reserve the right to exercise the authority in this or future conflicts.

George W. Bush, February 7, 2002

To be in New York on September 11th was a strangely out-of-time and out-of-space experience. The World Trade Center so dominated the skyline that millions of New Yorkers could watch first hand as the towers burned and then crumbled. Ash billowed through downtown streets and people ran in fear from the buildings, or else they ran toward the towers in search of loved ones. The flotsam of terror—memos, office stationary, resumés—wafted over the East River to Brooklyn. Delivery workers and waiters, money managers and secretaries, firefighters and janitors—people from more than ninety countries died that morning. For those who survived, inexplicable horror shrouded a sense of numb sleepwalking through evacuated streets. Work ceased, telephones were dead, and sirens slit the air; airports and tunnels were closed, the subway halted; the stock market was still, and television was ad-free in tacit recognition that amidst such horror, the continuation of capitalism as usual was too vulgar. Manhattan was sealed off. Time stopped and space was suddenly infinite. Any certainty about the coming seconds, minutes, hours and days evaporated. Where time moved at all it did not flow but rather convulsed as the shock of repressed horror periodically caught up with the moment. But you could still walk. A stilled Manhattan was strangely open to the sky as empty streets promised the endlessness of space against the closure of time.

For days afterward, as the monstrous "pile" of rubble smoldered above a white-hot core, New Yorkers' nostrils were seared by the acrid, toxic wind of incinerated cement, computers, and bodies. The city that styled itself the capital of a globalizing world found itself suddenly prostrate before global forces against which a hubristic America, its immunity seemingly guaranteed by geography, had not thought to defend itself.

"The world changed on September 11th," George W. Bush has said over and over again, "and since then we have changed the world." The first part of this declaration is not true. In and of itself, September 11th did not change the world. Numerous disasters, humanly inspired or otherwise, have been much more calamitous and claimed many more than the 2,900 lives lost on September 11th. But few such events have had such a symbolic effect as the embarrassingly simple use of commercial aircraft to fell buildings devoted to the economic and military supremacy of the world's only remaining superpower. What made the attack on the twin towers and the destruction of a wing of the Pentagon so exceptional was less its direct consequences and more its stunning ideological impact. It was kryptonite to the global superpower's sense of impregnability, shattering an immunity worn as national birthright. It revealed how utterly out of touch American leaders—and much of the populace—were concerning the country's hegemony and the contradictory realities of a globalization it promoted for its own benefit. The second part of Bush's declaration is therefore manifestly true. The symbolic impact of 9/11 was global, and the practical repercussions, pulsing outward from Washington, have been mobilized to rewrite world politics from Iraq to Iowa.

The US response was immediate (if we discount the seven minutes during which a befuddled George W. Bush, relieved of his closest handlers, kept reading to a class of Florida six-year-olds after being told that America was under attack). Osama bin Laden was quickly identified as the culprit. Photos of him overprinted with a bull's eye target sprouted in American streets and bars alongside the Stars and Stripes, and al Qaeda became a household word. With a Christian assuredness that would have made Woodrow Wilson blush, Bush announced a global "crusade against terrorism" with the Judeo-Christian West set to bring "Infinite Justice" to the barbarians of the desert. The twenty-first century AD, apparently, would look a bit like the twelfth, with George Bush as latter-day Richard the Lionhearted.

Visiting a Washington mosque several days after 9/11, Bush assured the world that the coming war against Arabs and Muslims was not a war against Arabs and Muslims. For many the war had already started, of course. Dozens of Asian men and women were assaulted on American streets in the days after 9/11, and a few were even killed in random acts of racist hatred as the faithful felt themselves bugled to action; police and FBI sweeps incarcerated thousands of people of South Asian and Middle Eastern decent. Meanwhile White House rhetoric shoe-horned world elites into supporting roles—"if you are not with us you are with the terrorists"—and the subsequent "war on terrorism" recruited enthusiastic support from Britain's Tony Blair along with more cautious support from elsewhere.

The first significant shot in that war, the bombardment and invasion of an already devastated Afghanistan, where bin Laden was thought to be, also revealed a breadth of popular global opposition as protests mounted. But a paucity of targets and a failure to hit them made Afghanistan a frustrating war for the Pentagon. Yet the real target had long been in the sights of the Bushites, evident when Donald Rumsfeld declared Iraq a preferable alternative: unlike Afghanistan, it was "target-rich." Neocons from the Project for a New American Century (PNAC) had long ago judged that US "containment" of Hussein after the first Gulf war had failed, and that Iraq represented the most severe post-cold war threat to "the vital interests of the United States." They implored congressional leaders and Bill Clinton, who throughout his presidency continued a low-level aerial war against Iraq, to counter the "threat of weapons of mass destruction." "U.S. policy should have as its explicit goal removing Saddam Hussein's regime from power.... We should use U.S. and allied military power ... to protect our vital interests in the Gulf—and, if necessary, to help remove Saddam from power." Among the signatories of this 1998 appeal were Donald Rumsfeld and Paul Wolfowitz, respectively Bush's Secretary and Deputy Secretary of Defense, and Richard Perle, chair of the President's Defense Policy Board.[1] From the beginning of the Bush administration this group had pressed for all-out war against Iraq but the President was unsure. September 11th was a gift to their cause and Bush raised the banner.

The pretexts for the Iraq war, we now know, were spurious. The threat of Iraqi weapons of mass destruction (WMDs) raining down on American cities was patently concocted in the White House and Whitehall despite intelligence to the contrary; the connection between al Qaeda and Saddam also emanated from a vivid Washington imagination; and any supposed concern for Iraqi human rights was a cruel sham in light of the deadly effects of US/UN sanctions after 1991, credited by the UN itself with killing as many as half a million children. We also know that those failed pretexts were not a case of intelligence failure but of intelligence suppression when unfavorable reports failed to endorse pre-determined aggression. Whatever the mix of devious intent and outright lying, the pretexts summoned for war nonetheless provided a spectacular if short-lived political success for the Bush and Blair administrations over the common sense of their people and popular opposition around the world. In the bowels of the White House West Wing, hours after the attacks on the Pentagon and World Trade Center, Richard Clarke, top National Security and Counterterrorism advisor, realized "with almost a sharp physical pain that Rumsfeld and Wolfowitz were going to try to take advantage of this national tragedy to promote their agenda about Iraq." They succeeded. When he finally got back to the White House that day, George Bush went along. "See if Saddam did this," Bush commanded Clarke. "See if he's linked in any way." "But Mr. President, al Qaeda did this," responded an incredulous Clarke. "Just look," Bush barked back. "I want to know any shred...."[2]

No shred was found, of course, but that was beside the point. The Bush Doctrine quickly took shape as Washington claimed the right of pre-emptive attack against any nation, group, or individual anywhere in the world that the US government decided was a possible future threat to its interests and security. In effect, offensive wars could now be justified at the whim of any president with a good, tax-funded PR team who could whip up enough fear to convince a majority of Americans that people out there were after them. That such presidential authority was approved by Congress, that the supposed nuclear threat by Iraq was non-existent, and that Democrats have nonetheless endorsed the Bush doctrine, not only suggests how dire the situation has become but gives a powerful sign that the so-called liberal and conservative wings of twentieth century American liberalism have come together in their bankruptcy. Without underestimating the huge anti-war opposition, it is clear that conservatives and many liberals, neocons and neoliberals, however much they may have squabbled about details and conduct, initially fell into lock step behind the war against Iraq. Never has Gore Vidal's observation been more apposite, namely that America has "one political party with two right wings." An ebbing moral and political tide apparently grounds all boats.

War against Iraq defied the very United Nations that Roosevelt had sought but failed to make an arm of US foreign policy. At most, the UN sanctions defensive and not offensive military action, and its Secretary General Kofi Annan eventually came to say what many others believed: the Iraq war was illegal and abrogated international law. The Iraq war also exposed in gruesome detail the contradiction at the heart of American liberalism. The delicate balance between claims to universal right and the particular interests of the United States, adroitly walked in the 1990s by Clintonesque neoliberals, was shattered as George Bush defended war in the Middle East with the claim that "liberty is universal" while over his shoulder the world recoiled at the brutal atrocities of Abu Ghraib, Basra, and Guantánamo.

A War on Terrorism?

Pretexts for war are never the same as causes, and post hoc justifications rarely tap real causes either. It may be convenient to think that World War I was prompted by the killing of Austrian

Archduke Franz Ferdinand in Sarajevo or that World War II was a principled crusade against fascism, but in both cases much deeper issues and interests were obviously involved. Imperial rivalries were paramount in 1914, and in the late 1930s many in the Anglo-American ruling class—from Edward VIII to Henry Ford—were not averse to fascism as a guarantor of social control, only they sniffed at its German accent. The same disjuncture between pretext and rationale applies to the so-called war on terrorism. Even as their successive justifications for war dissolved, US and British leaders attached themselves to images of September 11th, proclaimed Hussein the mother of all terrorists, and added testily that in any case the world was a safer place without him. The success of that strategy is suggested by a pre-election 2004 poll that found that 42 percent of Americans thought Iraq complicit in 9/11. The nightly news and morning papers were willing cheerleaders in this instrumental deception: while downplaying the fact that fifteen of the 9/11 hijackers were actually Saudi and none were Afghan or Iraqi, they channeled the demonization of Hussein as a substitute for careful analysis. This was true not just of the dominant right-wing press—*The Daily Telegraph*, Rupert Murdoch's Fox News, or CNN—but across the board. As the official excuses for war unraveled, *The New York Times* and *The Washington Post* felt obliged to apologize to readers for systematically devaluing or ignoring the abundant pre-2003 evidence that the Bush/Blair justifications for war were false.

To want to clear the world of dangerous menaces is a laudable goal, and Hussein and bin Laden certainly rank among the worst. But the justification for war, especially in the face of overwhelming UN opposition, is hardly so easy; besides, there are many menaces and terrorists to choose from. My Oxford English Dictionary defines terrorism as "a system of terror" or "government by intimidation." It defines a terrorist as "anyone who attempts to further his views by a system of coercive intimidation." That offers a very broad net. Who gets to call who a terrorist, who gets to have their definitions stick on the global airwaves, and who gets to initiate military action against others are hardly questions susceptible to forensic science but the outcome of intense political struggle, ideological wrangling, diplomatic blackmail, and ultimately force. Insofar as victors write the histories of war and arbitrate between good and evil, might can indeed be made right in the eyes of future generations. The very language of a "war on terrorism" expresses this struggle.

In the first place, the "war on terrorism" is highly selective, aiming at Arabs and Muslims but catching numerous others as well. While many innocents have been branded terrorists, others who don't fit the profile, yet are responsible for heinous terrorist acts, have often avoided that label. Even before 9/11, the US government and media writhed in discomfort about how to characterize Oklahoma bomber Timothy McVeigh, who killed 167 people with a truck bomb. Although seen as a "terrorist" by some, "bomber" was the appellation that stuck, and he was rarely if ever branded a Christian terrorist despite the religious, right-wing, anti-government, militia fundamentalism that inspired the attack. His opposition to the United Nations and gun control, among other things, might of course have embarrassed even moderate conservatives with similar passions. Since 9/11 an even more powerful association has been forged between terrorism and anti-Americanism, such that the idea of "American terror-ist"—unlike that of Iraqi or Palestinian terrorist—seems almost oxymoronic.

Conversely, had this been a genuine war on global terror it would presumably have targeted a broader range of those orches-trating terror around the world. Geographically closer and cer-tainly cheaper would have been an assault on the corrupt Colombian regime overseeing a paramilitary campaign of state-sponsored terror against peasants and leftist opponents under the guise of a war on drugs. It would also presumably have targeted the Indonesian military, similarly fighting various factions of its own population who are struggling against state repression. And it might have targeted the Israeli administration of Ariel Sharon, which has unleashed a "system of terror" against Palestinians whom it certainly treats with "coercive intimidation": since September 2000 the Israeli Defense Force has killed more than 3,200 Palestinians, many of them children and women. Terror on the one side is met by terror on the other: instead of tackling such instances of terrorism, the US government provides billions of dollars of military and other support to sustain state terror in Colombia, Indonesia, and especially Israel. At the very least, the war on terrorism is ideologically selective but in no way arbitrary.

"You can see a lot just by looking," baseballer Yogi Berra used to say, so who are those people terrorizing the United States? Hussein was a highly rewarded client of US military and financial support as long as he was fighting arch-enemy Iran in the 1980s; Osama bin Laden was trained and financially supported by the CIA, beginning with the Reagan administration, as part of a de-liberate US strategy to make Afghanistan "the Soviets' Vietnam";

McVeigh learned explosives during his US Army service, including the first Gulf war; the motive behind the 2001 anthrax attacks in the US is not publicly known but the strain of anthrax strongly suggests that it emanated from a US government or military-sponsored laboratory. It would be absurd to suggest that the US and its military were directly behind these and other instances of terror—of course they weren't. But "there is a connection"—certainly more of a connection than any discovered between Hussein and al Qaeda—a connection engendered by the foreign policy of a state bent on global power which finds itself consistently backing a "lesser evil." It begins to look as if the war on terrorism has had all of the wrong targets, pricking away at the extremities of a multi-headed hydra instead of hitting its heart and brain. It begins to look as if an effective war on terrorism might take as its first target a US military that has at one time or another sponsored so much of this rogue's gallery.

The ideological work done by the appellation "terrorist" is not difficult to discern: it describes a symptom while masking any sense of cause; it flattens all violent challenges to established states (at least those states characterized as, or supported by, capitalist "democracies") into a one-dimensional condemnation. Insurgencies against the "civilized" norm are pathologized, ripped from context or reason. The struggle for a Palestinian homeland, a united Ireland, an independent Chechnya, or the fight against a corrupt Colombian oligarchy, an equally corrupt Saudi ruling class, or a US-centered global capitalism become instances of a single sickness defying liberal propriety. Attributions of terrorism deny any legitimacy to violent opposition while justifying violence in response. As Osama bin Laden could amply testify, however, the difference between freedom fighter and terrorist has less to do with the behavior of any particular group and everything to do with the changing interests of the states and ruling classes that sponsor or oppose them: terrorists are defined as much by who they attack as how they do it.

The fulcrum on which definitions of terrorism are weighed comes from Max Weber, who identified the state as that entity which wields a legitimate monopoly over violence. If this is a true and broadly accepted definition of the modern state it does not actually tell us much, and it is even less useful in delineating what counts as terrorism. In the first place, it is a rather inconvenient fact that most modern states owe their origins to terrorism. The Terror of 1792–1794, following the revolution, not only established the modern French state but gave its name to contemporary terrorism; more than a century earlier Cromwell wrought a different kind of terror in the name of English and eventually British unity; George Washington's revolutionary army in the US was the ultimate terrorist apparatus of the day against "legitimate" British colonialists and their redcoats; Nobel Peace Prize winner Menachem Begin freely admitted he was a terrorist of necessity insofar as his Irgun successfully shot and bombed its way to an Israeli state; anti-colonial movements after World War II, from India to Kenya to Vietnam, mobilized terror against ruling states in search of a similar result. States without terrorist origins are the exception, not the rule. Historically, terrorism and liberal pacifism are not unalterably opposed: whether in France or Britain, Washington or Tel Aviv, liberalism came to rule not despite terrorism but as its sweetest fruit. In this light, George

Bush's insistence that "liberty is universal" has an ominous echo, a global threat veiled as crusade for enlightenment.

The war on terror in Afghanistan was a fiasco. Initiated on October 7, 2001, it dislodged a despicable Taliban government that gave bin Laden refuge, but in the process it bombed villages, markets, weddings, and civilians, killing thousands. For the Bush administration, war was necessary to "restore American credibility" but it backfired as the most technological army on earth could not find those whom Bush derided as "cave dwellers" (cartoonists around the world in turn mocked the American President as a brutish hominid with a chimp's intelligence). When after three weeks journalists were allowed to see the war first hand the social and physical devastation was evident. In one instance, angry, distraught women whose village had been bombed, their children and husbands killed, ran toward newly arrived reporters and harangued them: "Why do Americans hate us so much?" The echo of Americans' own plaintiff refrain after 9/11 was chilling, but it passed in virtual silence. As the Taliban regroups, the new US-sponsored Afghanistan is not so dissimilar from the old—regional military commanders refusing a puppet administration in Kabul. From the vantage point of many Afghans, 9/11 unleashed not a war *on* terror but a war *of* terror. American liberalism, for many, has replaced one form of terror with another.

Iraq, in turn, became a quagmire. Unhinged from any clear objective once the opposition regrouped, the US military flailed in search of social and military order, but the purported peace was more contested and more violent than the war. As markets, villages, weddings, and civilians were again subject to carnage, Baghdad did not turn out with flowers and chocolate for US troops.[3] Instead, the blend of arrogance and ignorance that spawned such a fallacious expectation hardened into quiet desperation. Falluja, Ramadi, Najaf—city after city became no-go zones for the army of occupation, and a hastily organized interim Iraqi government and police force had even less control. Any dream of "normalization" dissolved into the predictable prospect of an American-made civil war as hearts and minds deserted the cause by the thousands. The atrocities at Abu Ghraib became a forthright symbol of the depth of failure.

The notorious prison twenty miles west of Baghdad, Abu Ghraib was not a symptom of rogue soldiers undertrained and out of control but the product of deliberate policy that not only continued a sorry history from the Saddam years but more than any other aspect of the war exposed the contradictions of liberalism on a mission. The torture, beating, sexual humiliation, rape, and killing of Iraqi prisoners by US personnel at Abu Ghraib exposed the iron fist behind the rhetoric of enlightenment. A special section of the prison, known affectionately by soldiers and "contract workers" as Camp Cropper, held up to 600 "high value" prisoners at a time, dozens if not hundreds unrevealed to the Red Cross or the outside world. The most revolting thing about the torture photographs that stunned the world was not just their truth but their matter-of-factness: the US soldiers were laughing, smoking, smirking, pointing at genitals, giving the thumbs-up. (The photographs were revealed because soldiers sent them back to relatives in the US much as one might send holiday snapshots.) In one case they gloated over the body of a prisoner who was "stressed out so bad that the man passed away." Just a "college prank" was how right wing radio cipher Rush Limbaugh understood the horror.[4]

The US military knew better, concluding in a secret army investigation well before the photographs shocked the world that "sadistic, blatant, and wanton criminal abuses" were commonplace at Abu Ghraib. A quick campaign tried to isolate Abu Ghraib as an abnormal instance of irrational violence on the part of a few "bad apples," and this at least was consistent: terrorism again was pathologized. Military higher-ups played the class card, calling attention to untrained reservists—"recycled hillbillies from Cumberland, Maryland," as one former military intelligence official put it. But this deflection also failed. As military grunts were court-martialed and made the public face of disgrace, multiple inquiries put the spotlight on the top brass, the Pentagon, and the White House, and it became increasingly clear that terrorizing imprisoned Iraqis in a desperate search for information was routine and official policy.

The Department of Defense (DOD) had always had so-called "black programs"—"special access programs" (SAPs)—that reported only to the Secretary and his deputy, subvented normal intelligence systems, had no traceable budgets, and were often unknown to Congress. Frustrated by the cautious intelligence of the CIA and the inability of the US to trap or kill al Qaeda in Afghanistan, Secretary of Defense Rumsfeld dramatically expanded the role of these programs in 2002. The DOD was apparently flummoxed by its own propaganda, unable to comprehend the fusillade of opposition firepower that greeted the occupiers instead of the flowers at their feet that they expected. This was no mere intelligence failure, but potentially a total operation failure, and they knew it. A desperate Rumsfeld expanded the role of his SAPs: where did the unexpected opposition come from, what did it want, who was behind it? As the special ops personnel took over military intelligence in Abu Ghraib's Camp Cropper, the CIA wisely opted out, recognizing that instead of "high-value terrorists," they were now supposed to interrogate "cabdrivers, brothers-in-law, and people pulled off the streets."⁵ The CIA was not alone in its disgust, and editors at *The Boston Globe* agreed: "Mr. Rumsfeld should not just be impeached. He should be tried as a war criminal." As an Iraqi victim put it, "Saddam took our money and our profits and our life, and now the American Army is doing the same thing."⁶

How do the war crimes of Abu Ghraib and the larger war on Iraq represent a failure of liberalism? At one level, the answer is obvious. The scale of torture and killings obviously pale in comparison with the more notorious wars and other horrors of the twentieth century, but the justifications for American behavior go to the heart of democratic liberalism. Supposedly intended to depose a dictator, the war quickly turned into a vendetta against the very people victimized by that dictator, and the consequent abrogation of human rights and the contravention of Geneva Convention legalities exposed the naked power at work. As such, the American wars of the early twenty-first century highlight much about the contradictions of post-eighteenth century liberalism. To see this we have to trace our steps back to the template for Abu Ghraib: Guantánamo.

Guantánamo Conventions: "New Thinking in the Law of War"

Abrogation of the Geneva Convention in Iraq was neither exceptional nor accidental. Iraq was not a war on terrorism that got out of control but an issue of *who* was in control. On February 7,

2002, four months after initiating the war in Afghanistan, George Bush noted that "the war against terrorism ushers in a new paradigm," and the world therefore needed "new thinking in the law of war." In a presidential order of extraordinary import, Bush cited the opinion of Attorney General John Ashcroft to claim that "none of the provisions of Geneva apply to our conflict with al-Qaida in Afghanistan or elsewhere throughout the world." Accordingly: "I have the authority under the Constitution to suspend Geneva as between the United States and Afghanistan," and "I reserve the right to exercise the authority in this or future conflicts."[7]

With this presidential order, cooked up between the Justice Department and the White House in a way that offered plausible deniability on all sides—an order never made public until the administration was forced to defend itself over Abu Ghraib—the American President gave himself the authority to contravene at will the international convention that had ruled the conduct of war for 140 years. An earlier military order denying POW status for prisoners taken by the US military in Afghanistan—they could be held indefinitely and without access to a lawyer—was already in effect, and the 2002 presidential order fortified the status of the Guantánamo prison camp. US forces eventually incarcerated as many as a thousand POWs there, meaning that George W. Bush probably held more political prisoners in Cuba than Fidel Castro.

Wartime internment is not novel. Prisoners have often been moved a long way from the fighting—Italians incarcerated in Orkney during World War II, Germans in Oklahoma, and so on. The novelty of Guantánamo lay in the unprecedented legal void it represented. On the one hand, the Bush administration claimed that since the prison—known among soldiers as "Gitmo" —was not on US soil, none of the constitutional legal codes of the United States applied to the prisoners. On the other hand, the US refused to categorize them as prisoners of war, governable by international law, but deemed them instead "illegal enemy combatants"—a rhetorical invention of convenience with no international legal standing. In the doublespeak of Guantánamo, prisoners were both beyond any law at all and yet somehow "illegal," with the US claiming the prerogative to treat them however they chose. A social and legal black hole, Guantánamo pioneered the Abu Ghraib treatment. Indeed, in August 2003 as the crisis of the Iraq occupation unfolded, Guantánamo commander Major General Geoffrey Miller was sent to Baghdad to "'Gitmoize' the prison system in Iraq."[8]

In 2002 Guantánamo effectively replaced Geneva as the legal basis of American wartime behavior. Conditions in Gitmo have so far been less publicized, despite the accounts of several released prisoners, but they were bad enough to incite a US naval commander, defending Guantánamo prisoners, to compare George Bush to the scourge of the American revolution, George III.[9] The appalling story of one American *soldier* in Gitmo hints at the gravity of atrocities there too. In January 2003 an Air Force Veteran who served in the first Gulf War, Sean Baker, was asked to play a prisoner in a training drill at Guantánamo where he was now a military policeman. Placed in a cell, he was accosted by five soldiers who pushed his face on the cement floor, thrust a knee in his back and choked him. Panicking, Baker gave the code word to end the exercise but the "interrogators" slammed his head to the floor. Only when the soldiers saw his uniform under the orange jumpsuit did they desist. Sent to the Walter Reed Army Medical Center and diagnosed with "traumatic brain injury," he was eventually discharged. The military "lost" a video of the exercise, exonerated the attackers, disgracefully assailed Baker's credibility, and denied any responsibility. "If the US military treats one of its own soldiers this way," concluded journalist Nicholas Kristof— "allowing him to be battered, and lying to cover it up—then imagine what happens to Afghans and Iraqis."[10]

The American enclave of Guantánamo, perched on a peninsula in southeast Cuba, is a remnant from the 1898 war on Spain that inspired the American Century. Its liminal legal geography exploits perfectly the contradiction of a national liberalism redacted through claims to universality. It is a vacuum of legal rights, flooded with maximal power yet zero global responsibility, always *of* America yet utterly beyond its jurisdiction. Its legal status owes to the 1904 "Platt Amendment," ratified by the US Congress, which ceded to the new US-sponsored regime in Havana a modicum of authority in exchange for broad US rights of intervention. Guantánamo was part of the deal, a naval base that would let the US keep a watchful eye, and the revolution a half century later failed to dislodge this colonial anomaly.

Legal contortions over colonial Puerto Rico, grabbed in the same period by the United States, actually wrote the legal script for Guantánamo. Caribbean colonization after 1898 by the ostensibly anti-colonial power to the north was a delicate matter. American capitalists, seeking to avoid import taxes from the new colonies, pressed for the declaration of Puerto Rico as an integral part of the United States, but nativist sentiment wanted no further contamination of good Anglo-American stock by Caribbean "mulattos," and the continental US already encompassed a significant population excluded from equal rights— blacks, native Americans, Chinese, and others immigrants. When the capitalists' case for Puerto Rican integration came before the US Supreme Court, the justices squirmed. In a split decision, they eventually ruled against the importers with a truly solomonesque verdict: "whilst in an international sense Porto [sic] Rico was not a foreign country ... it was foreign to the United States in a domestic sense."[11]

This imperial justification of 1901 presaged George Bush's "new thinking" a century later. "Not foreign in an international sense yet foreign in a domestic sense" perfectly describes the legal DNA of the new "Guantánamo convention." A legal black hole, for all intents and purposes, governs more and more US state behavior at home as well as abroad. The Bush administration claimed that al Qaeda did not qualify for Geneva protection because it is not a state, fighters "did not wear uniforms," and they "don't belong to a military hierarchy."[12] Quite apart from the presumption of guilt with no option of proving oneself innocent, and whatever the issue of al Qaeda military hierarchy and the vagaries of battlefield sartorial choice, Gitmo prisoners were hardly alone in working without uniforms. Precisely the same legal limbo that keeps prisoners manacled in Guantánamo also applies to so-called contractors in reconstructing Iraq—freelance soldiers, security personnel, interrogators—but their fate is the obverse of Gitmo prisoners. Military contractors suspected of torture, rape, and murder in Abu Ghraib and elsewhere were not subject to US military law, exempted by a US order from Iraqi law, and immune to US law for deeds done in Iraq. While one class of participants without uniforms was incarcerated with no immediate prospect of liberty, another enjoyed global immunity; while some innocents were penalized as terrorists, some guilty of terror were admonished. The legal limbo of Guantánamo is no mere remnant from a colonial past, therefore, but a comprehensive and contemporary—albeit contradictory—strategy incorporating "a secret global network of prisons and planes" covering as many as twenty countries.[13]

For "America to remain a republic," concluded a Supreme Court Justice dissenting from the 1901 decision on Puerto Rico, "the Constitution must immediately follow the flag."[14] Full liberal protections, in other words, must be afforded people in all territories claimed or administered by the United States. The alternative, warned the judge, was a lapse into colonialism. Now the constitution manifestly did not follow the flag a hundred years ago, either in Puerto Rico or Guantánamo, and it did not follow the flag in Afghanistan or Iraq. The present danger is not so much colonialism of the old sort, meaning outright territorial acquisition, but a broader imperial assertion operating through the ventricles of global economic, legal, and military liberalism. That this imperial ambition has been forced to ground—quite literally to assert itself not through the niceties of neoliberal economics and multilateral legal conventions but through territorial conquest in Asia—signals not a continued expansion of this American-centered global liberalism but its weakness and impending failure.

The New Liberal Realism and the Bush Doctrine

Where rationales for war in Iraq were weak and transparent, liberal political commentators, philosophers, and historians quickly moved to shore them up. Many who saw themselves as left-wing—even radical—liberals led the charge. 1968 veteran Paul Berman celebrated the new twenty-first century "liberal American interventionism" as the only antidote to terror. For Berman, this involves recognition of the largely beneficent role the US has played in the world. It requires eschewal of the dead-end legacy of anti-Americanism that dominated post-1960s liberalism, and it puts its faith in a "new liberal radicalism."[15] British ne'er-do-well Christopher Hitchens was even more forthright, voicing explicitly (as the White House could not) the subliminal subtext of war: Hussein is a nasty man, we don't like him, just take him out, and quit the whining. Democrat John Kerry for his part pronounced himself more pro-war than the Republican incumbent: he would commit more troops, run the war better, make the world even safer than his incompetent predecessor.

Political philosopher Uday Mehta has already demonstrated the integral connection between liberalism and empire, and Niall Ferguson provides further historical context. He points out that Tony Blair's willingness to "overthrow governments deemed to be 'bad'" echoes the "Gladstonian Liberalism" of his Victorian antecedents. The US, he argues, long ago inherited responsibility for liberal empire, and with none of Mehta's ambivalence he advises that the US should learn from the British experience and, as a beneficent imperial power, grasp with humility its rightful and unprecedented global inheritance.[16] In many ways, the US has already tried to implement Ferguson's wish, as after 1989 it has taken up the role of global punisher, the terminator, superpower of last resort.

Michael Ignatieff, who directs the Carr Center for Human Rights at Harvard University, may provide the most eloquent statement of the new liberal realism. His book, *The Lesser Evil: Political Ethics in an Age of Terror*, implies that the old twentieth century liberalism is simply naïve, and its argument proceeds through a classic "on-the-one-hand/on-the-other-hand" format. However unhappily, Ignatieff says, coercive force is normal and necessary for "liberal democracies," but it must be applied judiciously. In times of terrorism, states may certainly overreact, but "emergency suspensions of rights" are nonetheless the prerogative of liberal democratic governments. Citizens' rights should not be trampled in the process, but neither can such rights impede the state's prerogative to lock up its enemies. Of necessity, it is cynics who run wars on terrorism, but that is justifiable as long as their doings are kept within limits. Wrong as a general principle, "torture might be admissible in cases of necessity."[17] It is regrettable but realistic therefore that liberal democracies must adopt terror to combat terror. For Ignatieff, the willingness, indeed the necessity, to use terror amounts to a "lesser evil" where the greater evil would be the threat to liberal democracy itself:

> ... defeating terror requires violence. It may also require coercion, secrecy, deception, even violation of rights.... To defeat evil, we may have to traffic in evils: indefinite detention of suspects, coercive interrogations, targeted assassinations, even preemptive war. These are evils because each strays from national and international law.... The question is not whether we should be trafficking in lesser evils but whether we can keep lesser evils under the control of free institutions.[18]

Ignatieff draws on John Locke's second treatise on government, in which he argued that a prerogative existed to act in the public good even "without the prescription of the law and sometimes against it." The state can claim such prerogative, says Locke, but so can citizens who have both the right and responsibility to "appeal to Heaven" in the face of repression and enslavement; citizens can "by implication take up arms to defend freedom." This was the argument that allowed Locke to support the American Revolution, of course, and it enhanced his political philosophy in the eyes of revolutionaries in the North American colonies. For Ignatieff, Locke's phrase "appeal to Heaven" clearly implied "that the armed defense of liberty was a lesser evil," but the "morality" invested in liberal constitutionalism prevented excesses: "morality" and "the moral order of liberty" provide a "depository" guiding liberal democracies in times of emergency.

The real question for liberal democracies, according to Ignatieff, is how to balance the legitimate rights of innocent citizens against the state's need to combat terrorism. How does the state weigh rights against the need for forceful anti-terrorist intrusion? Under conditions of "necessity," the doctrine of the lesser evil cedes civil rights to the state—always within limits—in the conviction that the greater evil of despotism can be preempted. Necessity never fully trumps liberty, but nor do liberal rights trump necessity. We "cannot accord a trumping claim to the public order interests of the majority" but rather "need to balance competing claims." "Liberal democracy has been crafted over centuries," he assures us, "precisely in order to combat the temptations of nihilism, to prevent violence from becoming an end in itself."[19]

A more meticulously assembled liberal justification for the war on terrorism—and the war *of* terrorism—could hardly be imagined. It gives wide prerogative to a state that decides, on whatever pretexts, to define its opponents as terrorists, and Ignatieff's lesser evilism surely warmed the hearts of the war's architects. Yet he is also defensive about potential philosophical bedmates, understanding that parallel arguments have been and can be made for quite illiberal purposes. He cites political theorist Carl Schmitt, who also argued that if the larger purpose was to defeat an extremism that threatened social disorder—he made the argument amidst the chaos of 1920s Germany—the state was justified in exercising power beyond the law. Schmitt's philosophical stance morphed effortlessly after 1933 into support for one of the greatest evils of modern times, Nazism, and so Ignatieff's concern is obviously justified. The fatal flaw in Schmitt, according to Ignatieff, and what separates the Harvard philosopher from his Weimar predecessor, was on the one hand a commitment to liberal moral order written into the law, and on the other hand Locke's sense that dictatorship rather than disorder was the greater evil.[20]

This argument relies very heavily on faith, however—faith that the vaguely specified depository of "liberal moral order" will somehow manifest itself, come to the fore in a fit of democracy and prevail over a state that cites security needs in support of a political clampdown. That outcome is not assured, of course, and adoption of the Guantánamo convention at home and abroad is hardly comforting. It is surely fanciful to assume that the strong state would suddenly see the Lockean light and concede that a little revolutionary disorder, threatening its own power, is preferable to a dictatorial state. The liberal realism needs to be more realistic by far. In fact Ignatieff defines the most central issue away as he makes "liberal democracy" the backstop of his case. The argument rests on the assumption that "liberal democracy" is inherently democratic when of course the central fear is that the resort to terror and the aggressive arrogation of global and local power by a strong "democratic" state subverts precisely the democracy that represents the last line of defense, the supposed moral rudder of this liberalism. Not just contradictory, then, this argument veers toward tautology: liberal democracy will survive because it is democratic. History, apparently, offers no alternative; Fukuyama's neoconservative claim of the "end of history" is, as he always said it was, the most perfect liberalism.

Ignatieff has unwittingly sprung on himself and the rest of us the trap that Louis Hartz realized nearly half a century ago, namely the danger of an illiberal liberalism, the irrational rationalism of a nationalized Locke. The danger was not what the majority may or may not do, Hartz argued, but the loss of effective dissent accomplished by a unanimous "Americanism." Locke's window of revolutionary possibility is bricked over in defense of the nation-state. Hartz was writing during the cold war, and insofar as Muslims, Arabs, and terrorists have become today's alternative bogey-men, Hartz's warnings are very real. The Bush Doctrine, according to which pre-emptive war is justified if a state feels threatened, has drawn support not just from Republicans but from Democrats, from its neocon architects and "new liberal realists" alike, and against this seeming unanimity, a powerful alternative to that doctrine is not yet in sight. Certainly, there is global opposition but no well-demarcated solution. The first step in creating an alternative may be to clear the terrain by challenging the politically paralyzing language of a "war on terrorism" and recognizing that this is just as much a war *of* terrorism.

The Bush doctrine of pre-emptive attack is dangerously self-defeating. It was already in practice in Palestine—Naomi Klein refers to it as "the Likud Doctrine" after Sharon's ruling Likud Party[21]—but now that it has been adopted in a blaze of moral rectitude by the world's leading superpower, it threatens to become generalized. In the wake of the Beslan schoolhouse massacre, Russia has invoked the doctrine too. Al Qaeda has already presumably decided that the American President is a dangerous man and the world would be better off without him too. As Iran found itself increasingly in the cross hairs of American or Israeli pre-emptive attack in late 2004, the Iranian defense minister claimed the prerogative of the Bush doctrine to carry out its own pre-emptive strikes to prevent being attacked.[22]

There is little sign here that a "liberal moral order" will rise phoenix-like to ensure good outcomes. By its very logic, the adoption of the Bush doctrine by any power automatically presents a threat to all other powers and would, under that doctrine itself, be seen as sufficient cause to warrant pre-emptive war. The result, should this "democratic" defense of democracy become generalized, is almost too hellish to contemplate in a nuclear world, and the biggest nuclear power of all would bear primary responsibility. It would not be Locke but his older contemporary Thomas Hobbes whose prophecy threatened to come true: the proto-liberal world of unbridled self-interest, Hobbes's *bellum omnium contra omnes*, a war of all against all.

7

THE ENDGAME OF
GLOBALIZATION:
AFTER IRAQ

No one has ever suggested that a single nation should range
over the world like a knight-errant, protecting democracy and
ideals of good faith, and tilting like Don Quixote.

Ohio Republican Senator Robert A. Taft, 1939

World politics shatters "Americanism" at the moment it intensifies it.

Louis Hartz, 1955

Shortly before US administrator Paul Bremer hightailed out of
Baghdad in June 2004 following the furtive wee-hours transfer of

power to the Interim Government, he defended his tenure as American Administrator. "Iraq has been fundamentally changed for the better," he insisted, with the country now on a path toward democracy and "an open economy." "Among the biggest accomplishments," he suggested to *The Washington Post,* "were the lowering of Iraq's tax rate, the liberalization of foreign investment laws, and the reduction of import duties."[1] This seemed a brazen piece of face-saving given the growing disaster in Iraq: gun battles raged daily, the number of insurgents burgeoned, the death toll mounted on all sides, and electricity and potable water flowed unreliably while the Tigris and Euphrates became sewers. Unemployment remained between 30 and 40 percent.[2] The more US forces attempted to quell the rising opposition, the more they made themselves a target, and found themselves ceding power in city after city to militias they had once vowed to destroy.

Bremer's emphasis on the liberalization of tax, trade, and investment laws over military pacification, political progress, and a rebuilt economy at this crucial moment may have been barefaced, but it should not be dismissed as a mere apologetic smokescreen for the chaos of reconstruction. Bremer's choice actually goes to the heart of the reconstruction effort and even more speaks to the larger reasons for war. His predecessor, Jay Garner, lasted only several weeks in the job primarily because while he wanted to hold quick elections in Iraq, his superiors had other priorities. Washington wanted first and foremost to privatize the Iraqi economy, thinking that security and democracy would follow unproblematically, and according to Garner they already had a plan drafted as early as 2001.[3]

The Iraqi Constitution prohibits the privatization of vital eco-nomic assets and forbids non-Iraqis from owning Iraqi firms. This would frustrate Washington's reconstruction plans, which put US energy corporations and related interests in the driver's seat and tilted less toward the preservation of national resources than to the ideology of a new "Open Door" for global corpora-tions. Further, international laws to which the US is a signatory (including the Geneva Convention) require occupying wartime forces to observe the existing laws of an occupied state. How to get around these legal provisions therefore presented the US with a serious dilemma, and solving it would take time. The Bush ad-ministration quickly set about appointing a "Coalition Provisional Authority" (CPA) which in September 2003 over-turned the existing laws on ownership. Bremer's subsequent "Order 39"—"a capitalist dream" in the words of *The Economist*—codified the privatization of state-owned resources, legalized foreign ownership of "Iraqi banks, mines, and factories," and permitted the complete repatriation of profits from Iraq.[4] The subsequent US-appointed Iraqi Governing Council, known derisively in Baghdad as the "governed council," ratified Bremer's raft of laws and regulations, including Order 39.

The awkwardness of Garner for the Bush administration was that he wanted an elected government too quickly—before the pro-corporate structural adjustment of Iraqi law could be imple-mented. With his removal and with "democratization" delayed, the US remained in complete control yet could claim plausible deniability insofar as Iraqis themselves had ratified the new US-written laws. As for Bremer, whatever the growing danger and mayhem of daily life for most Iraqis, he actually did the job he was sent to do.

Much has been made of the lavish US government contracts given to the Halliburton Corporation and its subsidiary Kellogg, Brown and Root. Halliburton, where Dick Cheney was CEO until his 2000 run at the Vice Presidency, was quickly awarded more than $12 billion in mostly no-bid war and reconstruction contracts but immediately fell under suspicion of corruption as billions of dollars of kickbacks, inflated pricing, and false invoices came to light.[5] Comparison might not be unwarranted between Halliburton and M & M Enterprises, Joseph Heller's fictional company in *Catch-22*, run by Milo Minderbinder who, because the bottom line was right, was willing to sabotage his own side.

Fueled by billions of dollars of US taxpayer money, the "Iraq racket" after 2003 provided a feeding frenzy for corporations woven into the military industrial complex, including not just military and energy corporations but industrial, electronics, high-tech, communications, security, and prison corporations, all with their own foreign "contractors"—a legal nicety for mercenaries, by any other name—despite the desperate Iraqi need for jobs. The resulting military division of labor in Iraq replicates that of the global economy: if Americans and Europeans were the interrogators, engineers, and managers, Indians and Filipinos washed dishes, swept the mess, and cleaned military toilets. Like Nike, the US military outsourced its operations. Its hiring practices are also suspect, leading one Indian newspaper to cite "US slave camps" and the Indian government to ban its citizens from working in Iraq.[6]

Halliburton is an agent—yet simultaneously a symptom—of something far larger at stake in the war in Iraq. A 2004 "Greater Middle East Initiative" proposed by the US placed Iraqi reconstruction in the context of privatized economies, trade zones, support for "reform governments," and the promotion of "political, economic, and social reform" throughout the region.[7] The operative perspective, however, is larger still—global more than regional. The nexus of world power and geography has changed dramatically over the past century, and the war against Iraq, camouflaged as a war against terrorism, offers one of the most explicit expressions of that transformation. US global (as opposed to continental) ambition, which first peaked with Woodrow Wilson's global Monroe Doctrine, competed with European colonial domination by resorting to a primarily geo-economic rather than geopolitical strategy. Whereas in the nineteenth century global capitalist power was pursued first and foremost through geopolitical calculation and the direct control of territory, a new Wilsonian vision had to be squeezed from the unprecedented necessity of economic expansion in an age with a paucity of available uncolonized territory. They led with the market more than the military. For Wilson during the first moment of global ambition as for Roosevelt during the second, geopolitics was far from obsolete. But except in moments of crisis (both world wars certainly qualified), stated US ambition was to displace the vulgarities of geopolitical contest—the "old diplomacy"—in favor of power wielded through the market. Geo-economic power supplanted geopolitical power. The blossoming of capitalist globalization in the 1980s represented a third stab at enforcing geo-economic over geopolitical power, and the Iraq war represents a continuity more than a break with that ambition. It represents the triumphant endgame of globalization. At the same time it exposes more directly than ever the contradictions inherent in this new globalism. The good news is that a predacious US globalism is destined to failure—endgame in a less triumphant sense. The bad news is that the costs of that failure could be horrendous.

Oil, Power, and an Alternative Globalism

"When oil is involved," laments Latin American writer Eduardo Galeano, "accidental deaths don't occur." Across the world the political left has argued that the invasion of Iraq was little more than a war for oil, and the behavior of the Bush administration hardly comforted those who would diminish the oil connection. Oil is a central calculation in any war in the Middle East, and the base of the Bush-Cheney administration's social roots—not to mention their individual and family economic interests—lies with that wing of the ruling classes in and around the energy sector. Globalization is a reality for this rarified global elite, which crosses national boundaries as a way of life and business. It counts among its members the Saudi rulers and the bin Laden family, with whom the Bush family shares corporate dealings in the Carlyle Group. (George W. Bush may be a curious exception here insofar as—incredibly for an American candidate—his utter disinterest in the world outside Texas made him a presidential candidate without a valid passport.) The priority accorded oil in Iraq was tragically evident as invading US troops protected oil fields and refineries as the nation's most valuable resource, while the National Museum, unparalleled for its collection of some of the world's oldest and most cherished treasures, was ignored and consequently looted. Questions of oil were always in view as the younger Bush placed Saddam in his bomb sights.

Access to petroleum resources has been central to US global ambition from the beginning, of course, and whatever the rhetoric of free market economists, its price and availability have more to do with the control of supply rather than any natural scarcity. The system of oil supply includes various interests: governments owning reserves can open or close the spigot; multinational oil corporations have similar power over refining decisions; and governments more generally affect supply via taxation policies and the maintenance of strategic reserves. "Peak oil"—the moment when the amount extracted from the earth peaks and begins to decline—will surely come, but when it does it will be the result not of absolute scarcity but of price schedules, transport costs, political control over royalties, taxes and sources, and the price of competing commodities.

In the shadow of British power in the 1920s, US oil companies had minor early "concessions" in Iraq, but Arabia became their true oyster after Standard Oil and later Aramco reached agreements with the ruling family. As it became clear in postwar years that the Middle East held the lion's share of world oil reserves, the US government and oil companies agreed with Saudi Arabia to provide military support in exchange for a US monopoly over oil extraction there. Elsewhere they sought to displace weakened British and French capital in the region while holding the Soviet Union at bay, most notably in Iran in 1953 when a US sponsored-coup toppled the popular Mussadiq government. This coup prevented the threatened nationalization of oil, re-enthroned the Shah and his military dictatorship, and established Iran as a major ally. An increased American share in Iranian oil supply was the reward. Whereas the US controlled only 10 percent of Middle Eastern oil at the beginning of World War II (compared to Britain's 72 percent), less than three decades later the situation was reversed: the US controlled 60 percent, more than twice the British figure.

The control of oil is not simply about ensuring the flow of a vital resource to the United States, however important that may be, but has a larger geopolitical rationale as well. The Japanese and EU economies are in a far more precarious position as regards future oil supplies, as is a dramatically expanding China. Enhanced US control over Middle Eastern oil offers considerable future geopolitical leverage to the US government and a bonanza for US corporations vis-à-vis their major global competitors. Grabbing greater control of Iraqi and other oil supplies tilts the global economy's playing field very much to the advantage of the US. It is not immediately clear how serious the threat was to convert the denomination of oil trades from dollars to euros, but in light of the dramatic weakening of the dollar against the euro after 2002, a US administration that did not take such a concern seriously would have been culpable.

But was war in Iraq really just about the geopolitics of oil? If so, why was it necessary to overthrow Saddam Hussein? Why did the US not simply work with him, much as they had done in the past—holding their noses if they had to, while Iraq continued to pump oil to the global market? Certainly Iraq's oil was nationalized, depriving US corporations of more immediate control, but that had been true for more than three decades. Rather, the war on Iraq has to be seen as continuous not just with the pursuit of oil but with the longer term political ambition for US globalism, an ambition that includes but outstrips any narrow concern with oil. In addition to the geopolitics of oil and the centrality of oil to imperial expansion, two other issues are pivotal. The first concerns the ebb and flow of US power in the Middle East. The second involves the shifting relations between Arab states, the multinationals, Islam, and western governments.

After World War II, US capital not only gained in economic power in the region; the US government also vied for political power. There was no shortage of contestants: emerging ambitious states in the region, Arab nationalist and Islamic movements, powerful and entrenched European interests, and of course the larger contest with the Soviet Union which cast a shadow on the entire region. For more than two decades the US saw its power rise, but it would not last, as a series of defeats reversed its fortunes. First, claiming pre-emptive right, Israel in 1967 attacked Egypt. As the US escalated military and economic aid to Israel thereafter, US political power in Arab capitals suffered. Next, the 1973–1974 oil embargo, following another Israeli war with Arab states, highlighted the realignment of power relations between oil producing nations, multinational corporations, and the world's major powers, and although exporting countries and oil companies profited from the fourfold price increase, the US government looked ineffectual. Third, the Iranian revolution of 1978–1979, piggy-backing on a strike by Iranian oil workers, eliminated a major ally as the US-backed Shah was ousted and the US embassy besieged. Civil war escalated in Lebanon, and under the cover of an invading Israeli army commanded by Ariel Sharon, hundreds—perhaps thousands—of Palestinian refugees were massacred at the Sabra and Shatilla refugee camps.[8] A US marine "peacekeeping" force moved to Lebanon, but after 241 US marines and fifty-eight French troops were killed in the destruction of the marine headquarters in Beirut in 1983, the Reagan administration ordered a retreat. This may well have marked the nadir of US power in the Middle East. Unable to keep allies such as Israel under control even if it wanted to, targeted by opposition forces throughout the region, broadly unwilling to intervene to resolve the central and most generative regional struggle, namely that of the Palestinians, the United States had failed dramatically in its postwar ambition to exert a controlling influence on the Middle East as a pivotal region of the capitalist portion of the globe. The ending of the cold war brought no respite.

Added to the geopolitics of oil and US loss of political power in the region, a third element helps clarify the conjuncture that precipitated war. This concerns the evolution of Islam in relation to the politics of oil. Hopes for Arab nationalism and pan-Arabism dimmed in the 1970s, but it is not simply that Islamic fundamentalism came to fill the void as it targeted accommodationist governments in the Middle East. Tim Mitchell argues trenchantly that western capitalism and Islamic fundamentalism are not so much at odds but have for the past century developed symbiotically. Oil money actually "made possible the resurgence of Islamic political movements in the 1970s." The role of Saudi Arabia is pivotal here. Oil money had set up the Saudi ruling class from its consolidation of the Saudi state in the 1930s, and the ruling Saud family in turn mobilized a branch of Wahhabists to help suppress

postwar labor opposition. It then took aim at neighboring nationalist governments that increasingly denounced the Saudi
monarchy and its grip on oil. Often at arm's length, the Saudi ruling family supported religious movements abroad as a means to
"promote its program of moral authority and social conservatism." The corollary is also true: the rising Islamic movement
supplanted the social glue and repressive authority previously
provided by colonialism: "political Islam plays an unacknowl-
edged role in the making of global capitalism."[9]

Where liberal accounts, from right to left, struggle to explain
the rise of "Islamic fundamentalism" as a profound "clash of civi-
lizations," a war against extremist Islam, or a softer instance of
"Jihad versus McWorld"—Islam versus a globalized West—we
should instead see a story of McJihad, as Mitchell calls it, an intri-
cate weave of political Islam and the political economy of oil that
was for decades mutually beneficial to the Saudi ruling elite, oil
companies, and various strands of the rising Islamist movement.
One need only think of Osama bin Laden himself to glimpse the
lack of contradiction between oil and Islam. More broadly, US
corporate power in the region always grew and developed in un-
easy unison with Islamic political movements and local states,
and rarely if ever supported secular democratic movements. So
what pulled the McJihad coalition apart?

There were many causes but the Gulf War of 1990–1991 was
perhaps the most critical. The devout Saudi Islamists who swelled
the ranks of the Afghan mujaheddin in the 1980s against the
USSR were no friends of Saddam Hussein or his corrupt secular
regime, but the ignominy of the US invading a neighboring
Islamic nation, separated only by the arbitrariness of straight-line

desert borders drawn in Europe after 1920, was incendiary. They were even more incensed that many of the US forces for this war were stationed in Saudi Arabia itself, a calculated risk by the Saudi ruling class which was also fearful of an Iraqi invasion. Osama bin Laden, having founded al Qaeda in 1989 and agitating in 1991 against the collusion of the Saudi state with the US, was expelled from Saudi Arabia in the immediate aftermath of the Gulf War. By 2003, so too, effectively, was the US military: American rulers were politely requested by Saudi rulers not to use their country as a base of operations for the new onslaught on Iraq—not that they didn't support it. 9/11 furthered this frag- mentation of the McJihad coalition, leaving in its place continued bilateral cooperation between the oil companies and oil-owning states, but with the United States government in an even more marginal position and with political Islam enjoying unprece- dented influence in the streets if not in the halls of power.

The rationale for the Iraq war emerged from the amalgam of these three elements: the geopolitics of oil, the dramatic loss of US political power after the 1970s, and the partial fragmentation of the delicate system of power interdependencies that let the re- gion's petro-capitalism flourish. The long-term loss of power weighed especially heavily in Washington in the 1990s. The win- ners of the cold war and the only remaining superpower felt they had earned global sway in such a vital region but were met in- stead with widespread disrespect. Nationalist chagrin reached fever pitch as Bush administration architects of war in the Pentagon and White House frothed about a "crusade" of civilized liberal democracies against terrorists, dictators, and a barbaric anti-modern Islam, which made for eye-popping whip-'em-up headlines but disguised a larger trajectory. Refracted through all of the rhetoric, for all its Judeo-Christian rectitude, lay the sense of a much larger, more menacing challenge.

Having lost its grip in the region, and recognizing the power of an emerging and antagonistic Islamism, Washington's major fear in the 1990s was that some sort of working coalition might emerge between Saudi Arabia, Iraq, reactionary Islamists such as represented by al Qaeda, and possibly other states. Such a coalition would fill the void left by lost US influence in the region, and if states bent to popular pressure, they would be drawn to increasingly powerful Islamic movements, leaving the US government (but not necessarily the embedded oil companies) out in the cold. The multinationalism of the oil companies and their increased independence from specific governments further weakened the hand of the US.

The prospect of such a coalition may seem far-fetched. Hadn't the Saudi ruling class expelled bin Laden? Weren't they antagonistic to a neighboring Iraq controlled by Hussein? Weren't Hussein and bin Laden in quite opposed religious and political camps? While a rehabilitation of bin Laden to his family and class might not be so difficult to imagine—had he ever left, and how did the bin Laden family escape so quickly from the US after 9/11 when all other air traffic was grounded?—a coalition between Hussein and the House of Saud is more difficult to conceive. If Washington perceived bin Laden as an intermediary, however, the unlikely becomes plausible. The real key in such a coalition would be the connection between Hussein and bin Laden's al Qaeda.

For precisely that reason, this was the connection that the Bush administration never relinquished when all other rationalizations for war crumbled. They always insisted against the facts that Hussein was "connected" to al Qaeda, even when no such connections could be produced and any Iraqi involvement in 9/11 was found baseless. Deputy secretary of defense Paul Wolfowitz provided the party line. His political training told him that war was the prerogative of states, and for him, as for many neoconservatives, it was an article of faith that al Qaeda could not have organized either the 1993 bombing of the World Trade Center or the events of 9/11 without assistance from a state. The state in question had to be Iraq. It just had to be.[10] For Wolfowitz, the conclusion was as inescapable as the evidence was non-existent.

Should such a coalition of interests in the Middle East have actually come to fruition, it could well have created a fatal challenge to the globalization project that carried US-centered ambition forward after the end of the cold war. War after 2003, therefore, was bigger than oil, much as that was a central calculation. Rather, a Middle East coalition of interests linking Iraq, Saudi Arabia and Islamist movements would have provided a significant threat to the vision of US-centered globalism that harked back to Wilson, received a booster shot with Roosevelt, and was again in sight with the advent of globalization and victory in the cold war in the 1980s. In each of these historical moments, the message was that might in the name of liberal democracy made right, and the only mistake in the Gulf War was not finishing the job by "eliminating" Hussein. Now the possibility of a Middle Eastern coalition sitting atop all that oil—spurred in no small part by US behavior in 1991—threatened to spoil the global party. The true target was not terrorism, therefore, nor even Saddam, nor just Iraq, but the perceived threat that the "Greater

Middle East" might consolidate a competing globalism that could obstruct the liberal democratic globalization emanating from Washington and New York, Tokyo and Frankfurt, London and Milan. George Bush has said as much, although of course his explanations don't come with footnotes to Halliburton's profits but rather drip with predictable platitudes through which the bare knuckle interests of American capitalism ride on the back of democratic babble: "Are the peoples of the Middle East somehow beyond the reach of liberty? Are millions of men and women and children condemned by history or culture to live in despotism?"[11] Translation: whether you want it or not, our liberal globalism will liberate you from your history, culture, and despotism: "Liberty is universal."

Endgame

Under the guise of fighting terrorism, the Bush administration mobilized the tragedy of September 11th to execute, in its own interests, the endgame of globalization. The world's major recalcitrant region, the crucible of opposition to a US-centered global capitalism, could now be put in the ideological and military crosshairs and brought to heel. The beheading of al Qaeda, unhinged as it was from state support, was an obvious and vital first step but Iraq was to be the ground zero for a broader conquest. But if its belligerent language and tactics were extreme and provoked global repugnance, neither its goal of a US globalism nor its strategy of bringing the Middle East into line was especially different from that of preceding US administrations. The Clinton

White House had tried to assassinate bin Laden in Afghanistan in 1998, and its UN-supported siege of Iraq was intended to squeeze the life out of Hussein's government. War in Iraq simply mobilized the excuse to do what Democratic and Republican administrations had long wanted to accomplish, however different their tactics may have been.

The transparent opportunism of the post-9/11 strategy lay not just in targeting Iraq or the Middle East but in the recognition that a successful US-led war not only delivered previously nationalized Iraqi oil to US control and provided a strategic advantage throughout the region, but relegated global competitors to the sidelines. Such an outcome was not lost on those competitors. In 2002 and 2003 French, German, and Russian leaders—and, had they been pushed, the Chinese—refused to support the threatened war, and this provided not just the necessary veto but meant that a majority of permanent UN Security Council members opposed to war. The opposition was hardly acting out of some higher moral propriety, however, but on the basis of the same geo-economic calculus that powered the Bush regime. France's arch-conservative President Jacques Chirac and Germany's social democratic chancellor—now turned neoliberal—Gerhard Schröder shared little politically, but both could calculate the loss of power to Europe in the event of a successful US military campaign. The potential Iraq reconstruction bonanza was variously estimated at between $70 billion and $100 billion, but military-backed economic influence throughout the region was the larger plumb. To have fallen neatly behind a US phalanx in Iraq would have consigned Europe—economically, politically, symbolically—to an even more subordinate role in the new globalism. Russian and Chinese leaders, with one eye on future access to oil but concerned too about broader geo-economic power, figured likewise. Prime minister Tony Blair quickly made much the same calculation but reached a different conclusion; with true English ambivalence about whether the country even belonged to Europe, he decided that second fiddle in a powerful trans-Atlantic coalition was preferable to a back seat with Europe on the global stage. It was a craven calculation. For this the British majority opposition to war gave him the sobriquet, "Bush's poodle."

That rulers in some of the most powerful capitals of the world opposed the US grab to consolidate global power in the wake of 9/11 should not be taken as a rejection of the larger project to impose a global capitalism dressed up as liberal democracy. Official opposition to the war, from Europe to China and Canada to Russia represented an internal squabble among the ruling elites of a capitalist globalization and a determination on their part not to allow the US untrammeled hegemony—a truly global empire—or at least to circumscribe the power of that empire. It was not anti-American as such but simply a determination not to let globalization become the same thing as Americanization.

Much has been made of the Bush administration's rejection of multilateralism in favor of a penchant to go it alone: it trashed the Kyoto environmental accord in 2001, dissed the Durban Conference against racism for its temerity in criticizing Israel, rejected the International Criminal Court because it would not provide Americans with a blanket exemption from prosecution, and mandated war with few allies and in the face of a global outcry. The adoption of the "Guantánamo convention" arrogated for the US the power to make or break international law at will. But such right turns from prior policies at best amounted to a tactical unilateralism. In terms of economic strategy, the unilateralists pushed much the same economic policies as prior neoliberal administrations. They aggressively sought free trade while trying to protect massive US agricultural and other subsidies to business; demanded liberalized capital markets while protecting their own with the power of the dollar; insisted on US corporate accounting procedures worldwide in a way that makes global corporate and financial transactions transparent to the US but not necessarily the other way round; and insisted on the global applicability of US law. Globalization was alive and well under unilateralism, differing only in that the partial interests of US capitalists were never so clear nor so aggressively asserted and the contradictions of globalization so obviously exposed. The thirst for war may have responded to neoconservative bloodlust, but the broader economic agenda remained neoliberal to its roots. As Niall Ferguson, historian and neocon fellow traveler, puts it in *Colossus* (a book whose title draws unashamed comparison with Hobbes' *Leviathan*): "the world needs an effective liberal empire and the United States is the best candidate for the job. Economic globalization is working."[12] American empire *is* the endgame of globalization.

The language of "failed states" is widely deployed to identify parts of the world outside the congress of global liberalism, states whose failures must be corrected if the global jigsaw puzzle of liberal democracy is to be completed. For reasons of corruption, authoritarianism, religious absolutism or some other form of despotism, such states have turned their back on liberal democracy and in so doing are deemed to have failed their own people and failed the promise of a peaceful world. These may be ex-colonies in Africa that have failed to "develop," dictatorships antagonistic to US interests, or Islamic states of almost any sort. With such a grab-bag of culprits, there is little coherence to the notion of failed states except that they have failed to progress along the proper evolutionary trajectory mandated by liberal democracy. They have failed to "pass go" in the game of global monopoly, stand in perfect antithesis to liberal American universalism, and must be sent straight to jail. Thus the description—"failed"—carries within it the vital if unspoken prescription—"need to be fixed"—and the language donates to US and allied ruling elites the right to criticize, blackmail, invade, jail, and ultimately to execute "regime change." The "only hope for such countries ever to become successful sovereign states," proposes Ferguson, may be "a period of political dependence and limited power for their representative institutions.... [I]n many cases of economic 'backwardness,' a liberal empire can do better than a nation-state."[13] The jail of empire is good for you. Invisible in this vision is any sense of state histories—their context, colonization, social struggles, or the role of post-colonial imperialism—or any sense of alternatives and choices beyond liberal globalism.

The endgame of globalization, seen this way, represents a triumph for liberalism with America in the lead. But it presents itself in a second, almost opposite sense that is far from triumphant. We can think of this in terms of what might be captured under the rubric of the "three I's": isolated, incompetent, impossible. In the first place, the immediate post 9/11 embrace of the US by people around the world was rapidly squandered by arrogance and aggressive warmongering, and this has left the

United States *isolated* to an unprecedented degree. At no time since the emergence of liberal US foreign policy in the early twentieth century has the US had so little support on the international stage. It was embarrassingly rebuffed by the United Nations, abandoned by several countries that had initially supplied symbolic contingents to the war coalition—Spain, Honduras, Philippines, the Dominican Republic, Norway, Nicaragua—and never supported by the popular majority of its main ally, Britain. So isolated was it even prior to war that it apparently bugged the European Union offices of friends and foes alike, including Britain.[14] With tens of millions of people in coordinated worldwide demonstrations after 2002, the upsurge in worldwide opposition to the US-led war recalled that of the Vietnam War era. Even in the US, sentiment turned against the emerging quagmire.

Besides the isolation of the US by 2002, one would have to add *incompetence*. The war on Afghanistan can claim to have displaced the despicable Taliban government but not to have eradicated the Taliban itself, which regrouped as US forces floundered and attention turned to Iraq. For those not hypnotized by mainstream US news spinning, war in Afghanistan was in almost all other respects an unmitigated failure. The prime targets, including bin Laden, escaped; hospitals, weddings, sleeping villages, and innocent civilians were bombed; some targets were bombed several times for want of new identifiable targets. After two years, the Karzai government in Kabul barely controls the capital and little else beyond as regrouping regional militias take aim at the US-supported replacement government. In Iraq there was no shortage of targets, but there too hospitals, weddings, and markets were among the places bombed, and the level of "friendly fire" was extraordinary: at one point early in the war more British troops had been killed by Americans than by Saddam Hussein's army. Incompetence was pervasive, not just on the battlefield but in the war rooms of Washington, D.C. The White House language of a "crusade" was a monumental blunder, bred of global cultural and geographical ignorance, which conveyed to the entire Middle East that this would be a religious war of Christians and Jews against Muslims. Even if the language was later retracted its effect was lasting. In addition, it was no mere dyslexic moment but a Freudian political slip of extraordinary political proportions that had the *New York Times* reporting, with nary a response, on the "Second Armored 'Calvary'" in Iraq. The confusion of a mobile US military regiment for the place where Jesus Christ is said to have been crucified speaks volumes.[15]

The Pentagon too invented its share of ludicrous schemes. In one, DOD Secretary Rumsfeld established an Office of Strategic Influence devoted to distributing "false news"—lies—to foreign journalists. In a less sinister case, the Pentagon planned its own futures trading market in which bettors could wager on the possibility of terrorist attacks and, as if media-generated US public opinion and American gambling habits established global truth—neoclassical economics on steroids insofar as demand begets supply—the military would use the ebb and flow of gambling traffic as a barometer of real terrorist threats.

The identification of an "axis of evil" was an act of supreme diplomatic incompetence, its true intent hilariously transparent. The world understood that Iraq was the true target of this vitriol and that Iran was being prepared as a later target, but North

Korea? In order to enhance the impression that nasty dictators with WMDs were the real rationale for war, and that this was not a war just against Arabs or Muslims, North Korea was hastily given a proud place in the axis. The axis of evil not only became the butt of immediate worldwide ridicule—the "axis of not so evil" was proposed, "an axis of almost evil" etc.—but it emboldened a defeated and decrepit Pyongyang regime to defy the US, assert they did indeed have nuclear ingredients and so what, and then openly offer and demand a non-aggression pact. An embarrassed US was flipped the finger, had no real response, but had to mop up an unneeded distraction. US allies in South Korea, meanwhile, were livid. Not only did the axis of evil suddenly present the prospect of new conflict on the Korean peninsula, but it abruptly re-empowered the North and scuttled an impending leveraged buyout by South Korea.

The third "I" is for *impossible*. First, world domination of the sort Bush has promised—"wherever there are terrorists we will hunt them down"—is impossible militarily. As he himself later conceded, "the war on terrorism is unwinnable." Still, the United States has an estimated 752 military installations in as many as 140 countries around the world and 2.7 million active and reserve personnel, of whom 400,000 were operating overseas in 2004—the most since the Vietnam war. They have a global recruitment strategy, with 37,000 foreign nationals in the military, and the number is growing. The US military budget of 2004–2005 amounts to $536 billion, including Homeland Security and the Department of Energy, but excluding the cost of Iraqi reconstruction. This amounts to higher military expenditure than the next sixteen countries combined. To put it in economic perspective, the US military budget exceeds the annual Gross Domestic Product (GDP) of India or Brazil, the Netherlands or Russia. Stated differently, the US military is the world's eleventh largest economy. The commitment of the US military to global dominance is unquestionable.

Whatever the military prowess of the United States, the promise of global military command is in the strictest sense a fantasy. With all of its resources, it has been unable to control Afghanistan, and 140,000 US troops have been spectacularly unable to deliver on the promise of pacifying Iraq, an economically destroyed country of only 27 million people with almost as many guns (many of US origin). Failure there is already apparent and growing.

The United States will also find global command infeasible in the realm of cultural politics. Many American headline writers confess they are shocked at a rising tide of what they see as anti-Americanism, not just in the Middle East but around the world as a result of war. For many in the US, this does not reflect the increasing isolation of their country but the wrongheadedness of the rest of the world which somehow, inexplicably, rejects the shining light of liberal universalism that is Americanism. Anti-Americanism there certainly is. As even senior intelligence officials have argued, nothing could have swelled the ranks of al Qaeda and other organizations as effectively as the invasion of Iraq and the subsequent deaths of thousands of innocent Iraqi civilians.[16] But the rest of the world does not necessarily live within the bubble of Americanism. There is a broad global understanding that one can oppose the warmongering of the US government without being anti-American. US protests about rising anti-Americanism are the mirror image of a deeply held belief in American exceptionalism and unchallengeable superiority. The street-power of Coca-Cola or Hollywood, Levis or hip hop around the world may be subject to transient fashionability, not to mention competitors, but is in no way inconsistent with an angry rejection of US global aggression.

The impossibility of US global ambition this time around may well be most marked in economic terms. The global economy is at best precarious. The US dollar—the world's "universal money" after the 1970s—is vastly overpriced, a situation sustained only by massive foreign investment in US Treasury securities. More than a trillion dollars are held predominantly by the country's major economic competitors, Japan, China and Europe, despite low interest rates. Their support for the dollar is hardly altruistic but a high-cost insurance policy that keeps US demand for their exports high. This in turn has produced a record trade deficit in the United States, where by 2004 it exceeded 5 percent of the GDP (an amount almost comparable to the entire military budget). Under the intense scrutiny of the IMF, any other country in this predicament would long ago have faced draconian economic sanctions. The plug would have been pulled on its credit. But the US economy is such a central pillar of global capitalist stability that a crisis there is unthinkable. And besides, they control the organizations that would discipline them. The exploding trade deficit is unsustainable and on its own could drastically lower the value of the dollar, but the refusal of foreign banks to continue mounting support for the US Treasury and the debt could have the same result. Either eventuality would in all likelihood push interest rates higher, and all of these shifts would combine to depress US economic growth.

The endgame of globalization as we know it, however, is unlikely to come simply as a military or economic whimper of empire, dissolving in its own impossibility. We can already see the same kinds of ingredients that were fatal to earlier drives for US global power. Those moments of US global ambition were defeated in full or in part by a combination of nationalist introversion and political opposition both from within and without. Today too the nationalism that lies coiled in every expression of US globalism has uncoiled in very dangerous ways. The mildest thing that can be said is that if September 11th was both a local and a global horror, its opportunistic nationalization in the US public sphere as a weapon of war has alienated the United States from much of the rest of the world. Other places have their own problems, and there is growing international resentment that "America's tragedy" is forced on them as the portal through which all world history and politics are now to be viewed.

In practice, growing US nationalism has many dimensions, but they are most visible in a sharp and rapid hardening of the national borders. Not only are ideas and images shut in or shut out, so too are people, capital, and commodities. American support for globalization in the 1990s was premised on the neoliberal belief that the global economy could be opened up while maintaining significant protections around the US economy itself—a "protectionist globalism"—but more recent US aggressiveness in its own interests has backfired, with the WTO issuing rulings against US trade practices in steel, cotton, and other agricultural products. In terms of economic strategy, since even before the

1999 "Battle in Seattle," the promise of a "new American century" has been challenged by a gathering coalition of anti-globalization, anti-capitalist, and social justice movements around the world.

The response in the US has taken various protectionist forms. First, successive administrations have protected American firms and corporations, using tax and trade policy to subsidize and shelter capitalist globalizing activities abroad while attacking the workers at home. Frustrated in their attempts to maneuver a protectionist globalism through various organizations—whether by negotiation or blackmail—while ignoring the reports of the deleterious effects of such agreements as NAFTA, they have resorted to bilateral and regional agreements—in the Americas, FTAA and CAFTA—in which smaller countries, shorn of global if not regional allies, can be bullied into accepting agreements favorable to US capital. Second, a broad array of "homeland security" measures has been implemented to inspect imports arriving by air, sea, and land. Mimicking the military, US agents, armed with Washington dictates, are setting up bases at ports and airports across the globe to inspect containers prior to shipping. "Pushing back the borders" out into the world, and simultaneously hardening them, is explicit US government policy. Its arm twisted by the US, the UN adopted an American redrafting of "the law of the sea" aimed at protecting the United States: it forces foreign ports to adopt US counterterrorism systems and procedures, makes them bear many of the resulting costs, and gives the US prerogative of enforcement. On land, delays for commercial traffic on the Canadian and Mexican borders have become endemic. Even in the financial sector, traditionally more global and cosmopolitan,

"America first" has become the rule, as the S&P 500 index has expelled numerous foreign stocks in favor of native-owned companies. A soft, fuzzy patriotic feeling this move might give, but an accurate pulse on a globalized economy it won't.

For individuals, travel to the US is more restricted, more expensive and more difficult than ever, with many travelers fingerprinted and detained, while border agents have been given the power to deport "aliens" without a court appearance. Academics, tourists, business people, scientists—in one case septuagenarian Cuban musicians nominated for Grammy awards, in another Yusuf Islam, aka pacifist singer Cat Stevens—were refused visas or entry. Countries from Poland to Brazil have retaliated, threatening to harden borders in the opposite direction. A decline in US science is already detectable as a result of hardened borders. US graduate schools have reported a drastic decline in international applications ranging between 25 and 50 percent, while the government subjects potential scientific publications to homeland security clearance. Severe restrictions on the traffic in ideas, images, capital, and people has a direct economic effect. US businesses report having lost $30.7 billion in 2002 and 2003 as a result of visa delays and denials alone.[17]

In 1919 and 1920, the nationalist rejection of Woodrow Wilson and the Versailles Treaty in the Senate was central to the defeat of the first thrust at US global dominance. In the 1940s, the Americanism that presented itself as the bulwark against communism, and therefore as an active precipitant of the cold war, may have drawn borders round a supposedly "free world," but it also drove a stake through the "new world order" and the second moment of US globalism. Today, for a large sector of America's rulers, the war on terrorism is the new war on communism, and the hardening of national borders—geographical, political, symbolic, economic—raises to an acute level the contradiction between global aspirations and elite, national self-interest. The new nationalism is self-defeating, and already boomerangs against US ambition for global command. If the Iraq war was viewed among its perpetrators as a step toward the endgame of a triumphant US globalization, it is turning into a different kind of endgame in which the nationalism within emerges to defeat its host.

After Iraq

During World War I, British philosopher, socialist, and anti-war activist Bertrand Russell wrote to his sometime-friend T. S. Eliot that he was not optimistic about a quick end to the war, and the reason was easy to see. The war will not end until British Prime Minister David Lloyd George has distinguished himself, reported a wry Russell, and that will take a very long time. The quagmires in the Middle East and south-central Asia suggest that we may find ourselves in a similar situation nearly a century later.

The primary tragedy of Iraq is that the American war was only secondarily about Iraq, and the Iraqi populace who suffered and survived Saddam Hussein now have to endure the American cure for a malady not their own. They won't be the last finding themselves in such a predicament. "Real men go to Teheran," was the post-9/11 mood among neocons in Washington according to one diplomat, and sure enough the US administration set its sights on Iran as its next target, the second node on the axis of evil, using the same failed excuses. Demanding that Iran give up the WMDs that he knew they didn't have, and subordinating international law to US dictate, George Bush insisted that "Iran must comply with the demands of the free world," and "that's part of the law of the United States."[18]

Clearly, the predominance of US military power makes this and other scenarios frighteningly real. Although comparable results might also be accomplished by more limited assaults—for example, proxy pre-emptive strikes from Israel—the costs either way could be immense. Neocons and others are fond of arguing that while US military dominance is a reality, the Achilles heel of US imperialism is the unwillingness of its populace to stomach all-out war and the consequent sacrifices in terms of life and lifestyle. America is soft, lacks fire in the belly, lives in "imperial denial," is squeamish about grabbing its real imperial power in the world. Whatever the truth of this, conjuring up a Romanesque imperial decline as the contemporary fruit of America's domestic decadence may be more than a little self-serving, goading "reluctant imperialists" to go for gold. "Real men" of the Hobbesian Collossus may yet step forward, with most of the world's nuclear arsenal behind them, to assert maximum force: "full spectrum dominance," as Donald Rumsfeld has put it.

However the military and political debacle of the endgame unfolds, the failing globalism of the US state is nonetheless increasingly apparent. The resort to unnecessary military might in the first place, as opposed to the common diplomatic currency of negotiation and blackmail, represents a major defeat that empire builders Woodrow Wilson and Franklin Roosevelt would readily have avoided. The costs of that failure are only beginning to become apparent: as bluntly calculable as the body count in the

Middle East, less tangible but very real in the "homeland." There the 2001 "Patriot Act" led the way in dismantling Americans' already eroded civil rights, but well before its passage, Guantánamo law was in effect as thousands of Middle Eastern and South Asian men were picked up, jailed, abused, deported, held without legal representation or trial, committed to illegal limbo. Powerful and focused as it has been, the racialized definition of terror could not hold, and antiwar and anti-globalization protesters as well as those opposed to Bush administration repression at home have also begun to be subject to illegal political surveillance and "preemptive arrest" aimed at repressing dissent and free speech.[19]

The clampdown at home is neither separate from nor at odds with the repressive nature of endgame militarism abroad. The one feeds the other. Front page news about terrorists "over there" rationalizes the political manipulation of the ludicrous color-coded terrorist alert system at home—yellow? orange! RED—cowing people from Wyoming to Arkansas into believing they are in mortal danger from a foreign or home-grown fifth column unless they lie down, do what the good President tells them, and spy patriotically on their neighbors. Conversely, ratcheted-up fear at home rationalizes the suspension of civil rights from New York to Abu Ghraib. Hitler's major strategist Hermann Göring long ago explained the procedure:

> [I]t is the leaders of a country who determine policy, and it is always a simple matter to drag the people along, whether it is a democracy, or a fascist dictatorship, or parliament or a communist dictatorship. All you have to do is tell them they are being attacked, and denounce the pacifists for lack of patriot-

ism and exposing the country to danger. It works the same in
every country.[20]

War and the fear of enemies abroad—real or otherwise—justify
repression at home.

Empire builders have always found to their chagrin, however,
that world domination is a fleeting dream, and in the case of the
United States there is a clear pattern. The first time around, as the
global Monroe Doctrine lay crumpled on the Senate floor in
1919, the "Red Scare" ruthlessly crushed domestic opposition to
US imperialism led by socialists, workers, black Americans, and
immigrants. Bolshevism was the threat, without and within. Yet
this opposition contributed to the failure of the Wilsonian vision.
The second time around, as the new world order lay breached between two worlds after 1945, Americanism also trampled the legitimate demands of workers and blacks against exploitation and
oppression. Again, communism and anti-imperialist insurrection
were the threats, and again, despite the expanded might of the su-
perpowers, the US fell short of truly global power. Today, at the
peak of the third moment of US ambition, Arab and Islamic terrorists are the new threat while anyone speaking against the so-
called war on terrorism risks being branded unpatriotic and
themselves therefore an enemy of the state. Administration warnings that the "war on terror" will be a long war should be taken
with deadly seriousness. When liberal political theorist Louis
Hartz observed that "'Americanism' brings McCarthyism together with Wilson," he could not have anticipated that this historical assessment would have such predictive value nearly a half
century later.[21]

If the outlines of an anti-triumphant endgame—the defeat of
an American-centered globalization—are already in sight, the de-

tails of demise are much less clear. Nor is that demise in any way assured. But in the wake of war's failure, the neoconservatives who largely drove US Iraq policy after 2001 have splintered into squabbling egos: while some refuse to concede any failure at all, others recognize the quagmire of Iraq, consider it a huge blunder, and offer dire warnings that a Vietnam scenario might be in the offing.[22] US government policy too is increasingly detached from programmatic ideological precision and more governed by seat-of-the pants pragmatism. The neoconservative moment has apparently passed. This is surely heartening news, but whether it will bring significant change in US global behavior is much less certain.

Insofar as US-fomented war in the early days of the twenty-first century was indeed about completing the work of political economic globalization, the differences between the ruling parties in the United States were more tactical than political. In fact, Republicans and Democrats throughout the twentieth century have shared the same imperial agenda while differing at times on how it might be achieved. It was Democrats after all—Wilson and Roosevelt—who capped the crispest definition of global interests in earlier moments of geo-economic expansion. Both parties then and now stood firmly behind an American universalism in economic terms, backed up if necessary by military power. The big picture laid out by neoliberals in the 1980s and 1990s, generally Democrats, is not antithetical to neoconservative world views but a central foundation of them. Where the neocons differed from their predecessors was simply in their greater stomach, even relish, for military power as the tactic of global choice. They saw the window of possibility and went for it. In defeat they will surely lash out, but they are also likely to sink back into a comfortable neoliberalism which, for all that it too has been under global attack since at least 1999, remains the core ideology of the third moment of US global ambition. Whether twinned or not with belligerent military adventurism, as seems likely in the short term, it is not so much neoconservatism but neoliberalism in decay that is the vital target for a rejuvenated politics. And this makes it all the more important that we comprehend the larger geo-economic rationales for war and imperial expansion—territorial or otherwise—yet also comprehend that globalization's endgame looks increasingly like failure rather than success. Without being too apocalyptic, it is worth simply noting that the Greek empire may have peaked when Alexander the Great died in Babylon—present day Iraq—in 322 BCE.

In retrospect it may be that September 11th comes to stand not as the beginning of a new phase in the American Empire but as its denouement, the beginning of the end for this particular moment of imperialism. Both prior moments of US globalism culminated in spectacular war, and although the first battle volleys after 9/11 pale by comparison, the third moment too is being capped by war. For the first time, however it is perceived, today's war is instigated by the United States. Isolation, incompetence, and impossibility together with rising opposition and a fatal inbuilt nationalism already circumscribe the possibilities of success in this war for US globalism. That a global American imperialism looks set to fail is the good news; the tragic news, of course, is that in the course of that failure, a flailing Americanism may exact a horrific cost in human lives.

"World politics shatters 'Americanism' at the moment it intensifies it," lamented Louis Hartz in his doleful defense of liberalism, and he is undoubtedly correct. The resort to a geopolitical strategy and war after 2001 represents a sign of weakness, not strength, for US power. The immediate prospect may be that the endgame of globalization will be shaped by the increasing fault lines of neoliberalism. In a neoliberal world, we are told, the central contradiction of power is that between the free market on one side and the state on the other. If the future holds a widely promised war on terrorism that itself embraces terror, this suggests a dire prospect—a world divided between state terrorism on the one side (the American-led "coalition of the willing," including Britain and Israel) and free market terrorism of the al Qaeda sort on the other.

Such a dire vision cries out for an alternative. It is not realistic to think that a self-defeating nationalism will, on its own, bring about a soft landing as the endgame unfolds. Historical experience tells us that such a nationalism, especially when it is located within the borders of a global hegemon, is just as likely to enhance rather diminish the violence of the denouement. That leaves organized opposition as the most realistic alternative to the clash of terrorisms. Tackling that clash of terrorisms requires opposition to war. It also requires opposition to the political economic interests and logics of globalization that fuel such an impossible war.

ENDNOTES

Chapter 1

1. Samuel Beckett, *Endgame*. New York: Grove Press, 1958, p. 82.

2. For a succinct summary of this history see Charles Tripp, *A History of Iraq*. Cambridge: Cambridge University Press, 2002, p. 49.

3. Elizabeth Monroe, *Britain's Moment in the Middle East, 1914-1971*. Baltimore: Johns Hopkins University Press, 1981, p. 17.

4. Available at www.newamericancentury.org/statementofprinciples.htm.

5. Henry Luce, "The American Century," *Life*, February 17, 1941, pp. 20-23.

6. Ron Suskind, *The Price of Loyalty: George W. Bush, the White House, and the Education of Paul O'Neill*. New York: Simon & Schuster, 2004.

7. Giovanni Arrighi, *The Long Twentieth Century*. London: Verso, 1994.

8. V. I. Lenin, *Imperialism: The Highest Stage of Capitalism*. Beijing: Foreign Languages Press, 1975 ed., p. 122.

9. David Harvey, *The New Imperialism*. Oxford: Oxford University Press, 2003.

Chapter 2

1. Louis Hartz, *The Liberal Tradition in America*. New York: Harcourt, Brace and World, 1955; John Locke, *Two Treatises of Government*. New York: Mentor, 1960, p. 343.

2. See for example: Bernard Bailyn, *The Ideological Origins of the American Revolution*. Cambridge, MA.: Harvard University Press, 1967; Gordon Wood, *The Radicalism of the American Revolution*. New York: Vintage, 1991; Joyce Appleby, *Liberalism and Republicanism in the Historical Imagination*. Cambridge, MA.: Harvard University Press, 1992.

3. Omar Dahbour, *Illusion of the Peoples*. Lanham, MD: Lexington Books, 2003.

4. Hartz, *Liberal Tradition*, op. cit., p. 11.

5. Ibid., pp. 11, 308.

6. Michael Ignatieff, "America's Empire is an Empire Lite," *The New York Times Magazine*, January 10, 2003.

7. Uday Singh Mehta, *Liberalism and Empire: A Study in Nineteenth-Century British Liberal Thought*. Chicago: University of Chicago Press, 1999, pp. 2, 10, 20. C.f. also: "One can reasonably wonder about the liberty one finds in Burke," Hartz, *Liberal Tradition*, op. cit., p. 11.

8. Michael Ignatieff, "Lesser Evils: What it Will Cost us to Succeed in the War on Terror," *The New York Times Magazine*, May 2, 2004, p. 46.

9. Mehta, *Liberalism and Empire*, op. cit., pp. 115-52. For a discussion of the "lost geography," see Neil Smith, *American Empire: Roosevelt's Geographer and the Prelude to Globalization*. Berkeley: University of California Press, 2003, pp. 1-28.

10. Nathan Reingold, *Science in Nineteenth-Century America*. London: Macmillan, 1966, p. 61; Walter Russell Mead, *Special Providence: American Foreign Policy and How it Changed the World*. New York: Routledge, 2002, p. 105.

11. Amy Kaplan, *The Anarchy of Empire in the Making of US Culture*. Cambridge, MA: Harvard University Press, 2002, p. 102.

12. William Appleman Williams, *The Contours of American History*. New York: Norton, 1989; Antonio Negri and Michael Hardt, *Empire*. Cambridge, MA: Harvard University Press, 2000.

13. Halford Mackinder, "The Geographical Pivot of History," *Geographical Journal* 23, 1904.

Chapter 3

1. John Maynard Keynes, *The Economic Consequences of the Peace*. New York: Harcourt, Brace and World, 1920, pp. 35, 39, 41.

2. Arthur Link, *Wilson the Diplomatist*. New York: New Viewpoints, 1974, p. 122.

3. Gore Vidal, *The Decline and Fall of the American Empire*. Monroe, ME: Odonian Press, 1998, p. 19; Gary Wills, "The Presbyterian Nietzsche," *New York Review of Books*, January 16, 1992, pp. 3-7.

4. Wilson is quoted in Senator Gerald Nye (R, ND) *Congressional Record*, 74th Cong., 1st. Sess., 1935, LXXIX, 8839; Senator Bennett Champ Clark, (D, MO), op. cit., 8837.

5. Warren F. Kuehl, *Seeking World Order: The United States and International Organization to 1920*. Nashville: Vanderbilt University Press, 1969, pp. 7-12.

6. Ray Stannard Baker, *Woodrow Wilson and World Settlement*. Gloucester MA: Peter Smith, Vol. I, pp. 235-243.

7. Margaret MacMillan, *Paris 1919*. New York: Random House, 2002, p. 95.

8. Ibid., p. 96.

9. Kuehl, *Seeking World Order*, op. cit., p. 4.

10. Quoted in William Appleman Williams, *The Tragedy of American Diplomacy*. New York: Delta Books, 1962, p. 66.

11. Quoted in David Steigerwald, "The Reclamation of Woodrow Wilson?", *Diplomatic History* 23, 1999, p. 84.

12. Williams, *The Tragedy of American Diplomacy*, op. cit., p. 93.

13. Quoted in Baker, *Woodrow Wilson and World Settlement*, op. cit., p. 326; in Link, *Wilson the Diplomatist*, op. cit., p. 149.

14. Keynes, *The Economic Consequences of the Peace*, op. cit., p. 33; Williams, *Tragedy of American Diplomacy*, op. cit., p. 52.

15. Smith, *American Empire*, op. cit., chapters 1, 6.

Chapter 4

1. Quoted in memo, Isaiah Bowman, "Leo Pasvolsky at Brookings ..." April 29, 1949. Isaiah Bowman Papers, Series 58, Johns Hopkins University, Ferdinand Hamburger Archives, Baltimore, MD.

2. Robert A. Divine, *Roosevelt and World War II*. Harmondsworth: Pelican, 1970, pp. 50-51.

3. Robert A. Divine, *Second Chance: The Triumph of Internationalism in America During World War II*. New York: Atheneum, 1971, pp. 84-85.

4. Eric Helleiner, *States and the Reemergence of Global Finance: From Bretton Woods to the 1990s*. Ithaca: Cornell University Press, 1994; Lloyd C. Gardner, *Economic Aspects of New Deal Diplomacy*. Boston: Beacon Press, 1971.

5. Fred Block, *The Origins of International Economic Disorder: A Study of United States International Monetary Policy from World War II to the Present*. Berkeley: University of California Press, 1977; Armand Van Dormael, *Bretton Woods: Birth of a Monetary System*. Hong Kong: Macmillan, 1978. *Proceedings and Documents of the United Nations Monetary and Financial Conference, Bretton Woods, New Hampshire*, July 1-22, 1944, Vol.1, United States Government Printing Office, Washington: 1948.

6. Jennifer Sterling-Folker, *Theories of International Cooperation the Primacy of Anarchy: Explaining US International Policy making after Bretton Woods*. Albany: State University of New York Press, 2002, p. 108.

7. Smith, *American Empire*, op. cit.; Hull quoted in Gardiner, *Economic Aspects of New Deal Diplomacy*, op. cit., p. 222.

8. Smith, *American Empire*, op. cit., chapter 14.

9. Sumner Welles, "Dear Friend," August 29, 1947. Isaiah Bowman Papers, Series 58, Johns Hopkins University, Ferdinand Hamburger Archives, Baltimore, MD.

10. Quoted in Turner Catledge, "Our Policy Stated," *The New York Times*, June 24, 1941.

11. Arthur Vandenberg, *The Private Papers of Senator Vandenberg*. Boston: Houghton Mifflin, 1952, p. 95.

12. Roosevelt quoted in Divine, *Roosevelt and World War II*, op. cit., p. 52.

13. Smith, *American Empire*, op. cit., pp. 27-28.

14. Brian Urquhart, "'A Great Day in History,'" *The New York Review of Books*, January 15, 2004, p. 9.

15. Williams, *The Tragedy of American Diplomacy*, op. cit.

16. Quoted in Bowman memo, "Leo Pasvolsky at Brookings ...", op. cit.

Chapter 5

1. Ron Siskind, *The Price of Loyalty*. New York: Simon and Schuster, 2004.

2. Edmund L. Andrews, "Budget Office Forecasts record Deficit in '04 and Sketches a Pessimistic Future," *The New York Times*, January 27, 2004.

3. Block, *Origins of International Economic Disorder*, op. cit., p. 203.

4. Helleiner, *States and the Reemergence of Global Finance*, op. cit., p. 135.

5. Gérard Duménil and Dominique Lévy, *Capital Resurgent: Roots of the Neoliberal Revolution*. Cambridge, MA: Harvard University Press, 2004.

6. See for example Helleiner, *States and the Reemergence of Global Finance*, op. cit.

7. Daniel Bell, *The Coming of Post-Industrial Society*. New York: Basic Books, 1976.

8. Robert Brenner, *The Boom and the Bubble*. London: Verso, 2002, pp. 31-47.

9. Rankings are measured in terms of 2002 Gross Domestic Product: World Development Indicators Database, World Bank, Washington DC, April 2004.

10. Amir Mahine, "A New Look at Trade," *The McKinsey Quarterly* Winter 1990, p. 46.

Chapter 6

1. Letters to Newt Gingrich and Trent Lott, May 29, 1998, and to Bill Clinton, January 26, 1998. Available at www.newamericancentury.org/iraqletter1998.htm.

2. Richard A. Clarke, *Against all Enemies: Inside America's War on Terror.* New York: Free Press, 2004, p. 32.

3. On May 19, 2004 a wedding was winding down in the village of Makr al-Deeb, close to the Syrian border, when US forces bombed the village and foot soldiers invaded. A doctor at the nearest hospital confirmed that forty-three people were killed—twelve women, fourteen children (under age twelve) and seventeen men (several wedding musicians among them)—and a video of the wedding documented the horrific aftermath. The US military promptly insisted that its operation had killed only "suspected foreign fighters," denied that any children died, and went to considerable lengths to make its story stick. A surviving witness described the events to a British reporter two days later, her hands still red-brown from the ceremonial henna used for the wedding. Mrs. Shihab, sister-in-law of the groom, had tried to escape with her husband and children:

    > 'We went out of the house and the American soldiers started to shoot us. They were shooting low on the ground and targeting us one by one....' She ran with her youngest child in her arms and her two young boys, Ali and Hamza, close behind. As she crossed the fields a shell exploded close to her, fracturing her legs and knocking her to the ground.
    >
    > She lay there and a second round hit her on the right arm. By then her two boys lay dead. 'I left them because they were dead,' she said. One, she saw, had been decapitated by a shell. 'I fell into the mud and an American soldier came and kicked me. I pretended to be dead so he wouldn't kill me. My youngest child was alive next to me.'

    Rory McCarthy, "Wedding Party Attack Kills 42," *The Guardian Weekly,* May 28-June 3, 2004, p.11.

4. Seymour Hersh, "Torture at Abu Ghraib," *The New Yorker,* May 10, 2004, p. 43; Steven Lee Meyers, "Testimony from Abu Ghraib Prisoners Describes a Center of Violence and Fear," *The New York Times,* May 22, 2004, p. A9.

5. Seymour M. Hersh, "The Gray Zone," *The New Yorker,* May 24, 2004, pp. 38-44.

6. Danny Hakim, "Iraqi Born Swede Says the U.S. Returned him to Prison for No Reason," *The New York Times,* May 23, 2004, p. 12; Robert Kuttner, "The Torturers Among Us," *The Boston Globe,* June 9, 2004.

7. Text of order available at http://www.kron.com/global/story.asp?s=
    1962000&ClientType=Printable. See also Richard W. Stevenson, "White
    House Says Prisoner Policy Set Humane Tone," *The New York Times*, June
    23, 2004, p. 1.

8. "People were escaping and getting shot" at Abu Ghraib, complained an ex-
    asperated Miller: Hersh, "The Gray Zone," p. 41; Tim Golden and Don Van
    Natta Jr., "US Said to Overstate Value of Guantánamo Detainees," *The New
    York Times*, June 20, 2004, p. 1; Tim Golden and Eric Schmitt, "General
    Took Guantánamo Rules to Iraq for handling of Prisoners," *The New York
    Times*, May 13, 2004, p. 1.

9. Jonathan Mahler, "Commander Swift Objects," *The New York Times
    Magazine*, June 13, 2004, p. 42.

10. Nicholas D. Kristof, "Beating Specialist Baker," *The New York Times*, June 5,
    2004, p. A15.

11. Quoted in Amy Kaplan, *The Anarchy of Empire in the Making of US Culture*,
    op. cit., pp. 1-7.

12. Quoted in James Ridgeway, "Mondo Washington," *The Village Voice*, May
    12-18, 2004, p. 27.

13. Stephen Gray, "America's Gulag," *The New Statesman* May 17, 2004;
    Andrew Buncombe and Kim Sengupta, "Secret Jails Hold 10,000," *New
    Zealand News* May 13, 2004.

14. Kaplan, *The Anarchy of Empire in the Making of US Culture*, op. cit.

15. Paul Berman, *Terror and Liberalism*. New York: Norton, 2003.

16. Niall Ferguson, *Empire*. New York: Basic Books, 2002, pp. 311-17;
    Ferguson, *Colossus: The Price of America's Empire*. London: Allen Lane,
    2004. Uday Singh Metah, *Liberalism and Empire: A Study in Nineteenth
    Century British Liberal Thought*. Chicago: University of Chicago Press,
    1999.

17. Michael Ignatieff, *The Lesser Evil: Political Ethics in an Age of Terror*.
    Princeton: Princeton University Press, 2004, p. 141.

18. Ignatieff, "Lesser Evils: What it will Cost Us to Succeed in the War on
    Terror," *The New York Times Magazine*, May 2, 2004, p. 48.

19. Ignatieff, *The Lesser Evil*, pp. 32, 144.

20. Ibid., p. 43.

21. Klein, "The Likudization of the World," *Rabble*, September 9, 2004.
    Available at http://www/rabble.ca/columnists_full.shtml?x=33960. It
    should be noted that this doctrine is much older. In 1981 the Israeli
    Defense Force bombed a nuclear reactor in Iraq, citing the fear of nuclear
    attack.

22. Elisabeth Bumiller, "Bush sees Joint World Effort to Press Iran on Nuclear
    Issue," *The New York Times*, August 10, 2004, p. A11.

Chapter 7

1. Rajiv Chandrasekaran, "Mistakes Loom Large as Handover Nears," *The Washington Post*, June 19, 2004.

2. Christian Parenti, "Fables of Reconstruction," *The Nation*, August 30-September 6, 2004, pp. 16-20; Adriana Lins de Albuquerque, Michael O'Haanlon and Amy Unikewicz, "The State of Iraq: an Update," *The New York Times*, August 10, 2004, p. A21.

3. Paul Krugman, "What Went Wrong?," *The New York Times*, April 23, 2004, p. A23.

4. Naomi Klein, "Bring Halliburton Home." Available at www.rabble.ca/columnists_full.shtml.

5. Elizabeth Becker, "Halliburton is Faulted by Pentagon on Accounts," *The New York Times*, August 12, 2004.

6. David Rohde, "Indians Who Worked in Iraq Complain of Exploitation," *The New York Times*, May 6, 2004, p. A18.

7. Steven R. Weisman and Neil MacFarquhar, "US Plans for Mideast Reform Draws Ire of Arab Leaders," *The New York Times*, February 27, 2004.

8. The Israelis claim a figure of 700-800 while Palestinians put the number at 3,000-3,500.

9. Timothy Mitchell, "McJihad: Islam in the US Global Order," *Social Text* 73, 2002, pp. 1-18; see also Rashid Khalidi, *Resurrecting Empire: Western Footprints and America's Perilous Path in the Middle East.* Boston: Beacon, 2004.

10. Clarke, *Against All Enemies*, p. 30.

11. Quoted in Jonathan Freedland, "The West's Arab Racket," *The Guardian Weekly*, July 9-15, 2004, p. 5.

12. Niall Ferguson, *Colossus: The Price of America's Empire.* New York: Penguin, 2004, p. 301.

13. Ibid., pp. 170, 198.

14. Elaine Sciolino, "Europe Union Finds Bugging of Offices of 5 Nations," *The New York Times*, March 20, 2004.

15. Edward Wong, "An Iraqi Factory Reflects US Recovery Strategy," *The New York Times*, February 15, 2004, p. 16.

16. Anonymous, *Imperial Hubris: Why the West is Losing the War on Terror.* Dulles, VA: Brassey's Inc, 2004.

17. Elena Lappin, "Your Country is Safe From Me," *The New York Times Book Review*, July 4, 2004, p. 11.

18. Elisabeth Bumiller, "Bush Sees Joint World effort to Press Iran on Nuclear Issue," *The New York Times*, August 10, 2004, p. A11; "All Things Considered, National Public Radio, August 9, 2004.

19. The Secretary of education called the country's teachers and their largest union part of a "terrorist organization": Robert Pear, "Education Chief Calls Union 'Terrorist', then Recants," *The New York Times,* February 24, 2004, p. A20.

20. Quoted in Gustave Gilbert's *Nuremberg Diary* from April 18, 1946. Gustave Gilbert, *Nuremberg Diary.* New York: Da Capo Press, 1995.

21. Louis Hartz, *The Liberal Tradition in America,* op. cit., 1955, 13.

22. Francis Fukuyama, "The Neoconservative Moment," *National Interest* 76, 2004, 57-68.

INDEX

A

Abu Ghraib, 162-164, 165, 168–169
Adams, Brooks, 41
Adams, Henry, 41
AFL-CIO, 117
Afghanistan, vii, 10, 13, 50, 149, 152,
    158, 161, 163, 165, 169, 192,
    196, 199
    mujaheddin in, 187
Africa, sub-Saharan,18, 50, 66, 68,
    114, 118
African Americans, 47, 80, 118, 168
Al Qaeda, 10, 152, 153, 154, 163, 165,
    168, 175, 188, 189–190, 191,
    199
Alaska, 103
Alcoa, 21
Alexander the Great, 209
Americanism, 8–11, 12, 15, 30–36, 43,
    53, 76, 78, 126, 174, 199, 203,
    207, 210
Anglo-Persian Oil Co.[BP], 6
Annan, Kofi, 155
anthrax attacks (2001), 159
Anti-Americanism, 11, 157–158, 170,
    199–200
anti-globalization movement
    (see global social justice
    movement)
Aramco Corp., 115, 183
Arbenz, Jacobo, 119–120
Argentina, 102–103
Armey, Dick, 145

Arrighi, Giovanni, 22–23
Ashcroft, John, 165
Asia, 18, 41, 62, 78, 99, 134
    industrial revolution in, 131–132,
    136–137
    Southeast, 114, 115, 118
Atlantic Charter,   98
axis of evil, 197–198
Azerbaijan, 24

B

Baker, Sean, 166–167
Bangladesh, 132
Bank for International Settlements,
    91, 130
Bechtel Corp., 21
Begin, Menachem, 160
Bell, Daniel, 136
Berman, Paul, 170
Bermuda, 92
Berra, Yogi, 158
bin Laden, family, 182, 189, 192
bin Laden, Osama, 151–152, 156, 158,
    159–160, 161, 187, 188, 196
Blair, Tony, 40, 55, 152, 154, 170, 193
Bosnia, 9, 147
Boston police strike (1919), 79
bourgeoisie, 37
Bowman, Isaiah, 99, 109
Brazil, 13, 14, 49, 107, 137, 203
Bremer, Paul, 177–180
Bretton Woods, 83, 90, 94, 95, 96, 100,
    110, 126–128, 129, 135

Britain, 18, 23, 42, 48, 49, 50, 51,
    63–65, 71, 92–94, 100–107,
    112, 115
  economy of, 128, 130, 133, 134
  in Iraq, 3–7, 183–184, 196
  as rentier state, 23
Browder, Earl, 117
Bulgaria, 115
Burke, Edmund, 42
Bush Doctrine, 154, 170, 174–176
Bush, Jeb, 19,
Bush, George W., viii, 20, 25, 34, 40,
    51, 83, 84, 122–122, 149,
    151–155
  and abrogation of Geneva
    convention, 149, 164–166,
    194, 204–205
  administration of, 7, 10, 11, 18,
    23–25, 27, 58, 97, 154, 182
  incompetence in, 196–198
  neoliberalism of, 194
  and Woodrow Wilson, 53–55, 76
Bush, George W. H., 19, 29, 97, 123,
    147, 182
Byelorussia, 103, 107

C

Canada, 40, 48, 49, 202
Caribbean, 48, 78, 92
Carlyle Group, 182
Carter administration, 132, 133
Catch 22, 180
Central America 48, 78
Central American Free Trade
    Agreement (CAFTA), 202
Cheney, Dick, 19, 21, 122 –123, 147,
    180
China, 13, 14, 24, 49, 50, 92, 100,
    105–106, 111, 114, 115, 118,
    120, 124, 127, 132, 137, 184,
    192, 200
Chirac, Jacques, 192
Church, Frederic E., 45, 46

Churchill, Winston, 5, 98, 104,
    105–106
CIA, 158, 163–164
Clarke, Richard, 154
class, 16, 38, 143, 163
  capitalist, 20–22, 24, 32
  struggle,37–39, 79–80, 117, 126,
    143–145, 147
Clemenceau, Georges, 57, 64
Clinton, Bill, 16, 20–21, 40, 51, 84,
    123, 145–146
  administration of, 13, 20–21,
    23–25, 27, 40, 58, 192
cold war, 8, 18, 96, 103, 111, 116, 117,
    124, 186, 188, 190, 203
  as failure of liberalism, 113, 120
Colombia, 158
colonialism, 25, 26, 41–2, 47–51, 66,
    67, 70, 114, 181, 187
communism, 29, 105, 106, 117, 203,
    207
Council on Foreign Relations, 16, 90,
    99
Cromwell, Oliver, 160
Crucé, Émeric, 68
Cuba, 14, 47, 71, 120, 167
Czechoslovakia,   115

D

Dahbour, Omar, 33–34
Davos, 83
de Gaulle, Charles, 106
Debs, Eugene, 37–38, 39
decolonization, 118, 127
deficits, federal, 122, 128
  trade, 128–129, 130–131, 200
  deindustrialization, 136
Democratic Party, vii, viii, 21, 77,
    154, 174, 208
Denby, Charles, 70
Denmark, 49
Depression, 91
diplomacy, 181

new, 56, 57
Divine, Robert, 88
Dominican Republic, 196
DuBois, W.E.B., 53, 68, 80, 111–112
Dumbarton Oaks Conference,
    100–102
Duménil, Gérard, 134
Durban race summit (2001), 20, 193

E

East St. Louis massacre (1917), 80
economic crisis, 48, 91, 128–131
    Asian 13,
Edward VIII, 156
Egypt, 185
Eliot, T.S., 204
Emerson, Ralph W., 45
Enlightenment, 17, 30, 43, 44, 75
Ethiopia, 68
Eurodollar market, 131
Europe, 18, 24, 29, 62, 74, 89, 99, 106,
    131, 137, 192–193, 200
    Eastern, 40–41, 115, 120, 124
European Union, 13, 14–15, 184, 196

F

failed states, 194–195
Faisal, King 5
fascism, 29, 81, 156, 173
Ferdinand, Archduke, 155–156
Ferguson, Niall, 170–171, 194, 195
feudalism, 29, 32
Ford, Henry, 156
Fordism, 138, 139
Fourteen Points, the, 56, 63, 66, 73,
    98
France, 4, 6, 11, 23, 63–64, 65, 67, 71,
    85, 97, 114, 118, 183, 192
    UN veto of, 97, 105–107
    Vichy government of, 106–107
Free Trade Area of the Americas
    (FTAA), 14, 15, 202

Friedman, Milton, 142, 146
Fukuyama, Francis, 125, 174

G

Galeano, Eduardo, 182
Garner, Jay, 178, 179
Gates, Bill, 34
gender, 32, 85
General Agreement on Tariffs and
    Trades (GATT), 84
Geneva convention, 149, 164–165,
    179
Geo-economics, 24, 50–51, 70–71,
    76–78, 81, 97, 147, 192, 208
geography, 44–52
    of globalization, 51
    lost, 44, 50–51, 212
geopolitics, 19, 50–51, 71, 76–78, 81,
    87, 97, 104, 147, 181, 184
Germany, 4, 11, 23, 30, 48, 59, 62, 64,
    71, 75, 87 , 97, 98, 100, 102,
    117, 127, 133, 173, 192
global social justice movement, 15,
    35, 82–83, 97, 196, 202, 206
globalization, vii 15–16, 22, 25–26,
    34, 44, 46, 51, 83, 84, 90,
    123–148, 181, 182, 190
    and democracy, 123
    endgame of, viii, 2, 11, 26, 27,
    182, 191–204, 205–210
    and finance capital, 128–136, 140,
    141
    ideology of, 142–148
    and production capital, 136–141
    utopianism of, 125
gold standard, 91, 95, 128–129, 134
Göring, Herman, 206–207
Granada, 147
Greece, 116
Gromyko, A, 102
Guantánamo law, ix, 164–169, 193,
    206
Guatamala, 119–120

Gulf War (1991),   84, 154, 158, 187,
190

H
Haiti,48, 60, 79
Halliburton Corp., 19, 21, 180–181,
191
Hapsburg Empire, 75
Hardt, Michael, 51,
Harlem, 118
Hartz, Louis, 28, 31, 33–35, 41, 43,
52, 149, 174, 177, 207, 210
Hawaii, 47, 103
Hayek, Friedrich, 142, 146
Hearst, William R., 91
Heller, Joseph, 180
Hiroshima, 113
Hitchens, Christopher, 170
Hitler, Adolf, 109
Ho Chi Minh, 67–68, 118
Hobbes, Thomas, 31, 34–35, 43, 146,
175–176, 194, 205
Holocaust, 114
Homeland Security, 76, 202
Honduras, 65, 74, 196
Hong Kong, 132
House, Edward (colonel), 68
Housing Acts (1949, 1954), 127
Hull, Cordell, 98, 99, 104
Hume, David, 30–31, 34–35
Hungary, 115
Hussein, Saddam 1, 16, 24, 26, 30,
153, 154, 156, 158, 164, 184,
187, 189–190, 204

I
idealism,
vis à vis realism, 55–61
and foreign policy, 58–61, 65–66,
67, 68, 72, 74, 89
Ignatieff, Michael, 41, 43, 171–174

imperialism, 6, 7, 18–19, 23–27, 28,
44, 67, 74, 156
British, 49, 50, 51, 70, 74, 170
confusion with colonialism, 42,
47
free market, 50, 77
opposition to, 109, 118–120, 160
theories of, 24–26
India, 68, 118, 132, 137
Indonesia, 118, 132, 158
Inquiry, the, 66
International Criminal Court (ICC),
20, 193
International Labour Organization,
64
International Monetary Fund (IMF),
13, 29, 41, 83, 94–95, 97,
128, 130, 131, 133, 142, 143,
144, 145, 200
Iran, 6, 132, 158, 175, 183–184, 185,
197, 204–205
Iraq, 1–7, 156, 177–192, 195–199,
204
(*see* also, Abu Ghraib)
borders of, 6
interim government of, 4, 162,
177–178, 179
history of, 3–7, 183
oil in, 24, 182–185
reconstruction plan for, 177–181
War, vii, viii, 1–2, 13, 24, 41–2, 43,
50, 55, 71, 77, 97, 122, 147,
152–164, 188–191, 195–199
contract workers in, 168–169, 180
opposition to, 196
WMDs in, 153
Irish Republican Army, 68
Islam,
political movements of, 185,
186–7, 189–191
Islam, Yusuf (aka Cat Stevens), 203
isolationists, 64–65, 87, 88

Israel, 12, 112, 115, 158, 160, 175, 185, 205
Italy, 30, 54, 59, 71, 115, 142

J

Japan, 14, 24, 49, 67, 80, 87, 100, 114, 118, 127, 131, 133, 137, 184, 200
Japanese Americans, 39
Jefferson, Thomas, 45, 85
Jordan, 4, 6
Justice department, 165

K

Kant, Immanuel, 30–32, 35, 45, 63
Kaplan, Amy 48
Kautsky, Karl, 25
Kazakhstan, 24
Kennedy, John F., 8
Kerry, John, 25, 170
Keynes, John M., 57–8, 59, 67, 74, 92, 94, 123, 142, 146
Klein, Naomi, 175
Kohl, Helmut, 29, 142
Kondratieff, Nikolai, 22
Korea, 67
    North, 197–198
    South, 114, 120, 132, 137, 198
    war in, 111, 127
Kosovo, 9, 147
Kristof, Nicholas, 167
Kurds, the, 3, 5–6
Kuwait, 4
Kuznets, Simon, 22
Kyoto environmental accord, 20, 193

L

Labour Party (UK), 39–40, 142
Latin America, 18, 29, 41, 65, 69, 103, 114, 137

League of Nations, 3, 6, 39, 54, 59, 61–68, 69, 70, 72, 74, 75, 77–78, 79, 80, 81, 87, 89, 91, 105
    veto power of, 101
Lebanon, 185–186
Lebensraum, American, 109
Lenin, Vladimir, 24, 117
Lévy, Dominique, 134
Lewis and Clark trek, 45
liberalism, viii, ix, 13, 28–52, 86, 94, 146
    as antidote to socialism, 37–39, 146
    conceit of, 61
    and relation to conservatism, 17, 28–31, 34, 36–44, 52, 60, 146, 154–155, 162, 173–174
    bankruptcy of, ix, 154–155
    classical, 17, 29
    contradictions of, ix, 32–3, 43, 56–59, 112–113, 155, 164, 173–175
    as expressed in Guantánamo, 164, 167
    and Enlightenment, 30–36, 43, 47
    Gladstonian, 170
    and globalization, 51–52
    and imperialism, 36–44, 63, 73, 170, 195
    and individualism, 30–34
    and nationalism, 30–36, 112–113
    at Paris, 54–56, 72
    and terrorism, 160–161, 170–176
    twentieth century, 29–30, 36–37, 38–42, 47–48, 55, 60–61, 143–144, 146, 171
    and UN, 112–113
Liberal Democratic Party (UK), 39–40
Limbaugh, Rush, 162
Link, Arthur, 58
Lippmann, Walter, 103

Lloyd George, David, 57, 64, 204
Locke, John, 1–33, 35, 42, 45, 70, 72,
        96, 145, 146, 149, 172,
        173–174, 175
Lodge, Henry C., 60
Louisiana Purchase, 45
Luce, Henry, 18, 108–109

M

Mackinder, Halford, 51
MacMillan, Margaret, 64
Malaysia, 132
Manchuria, 114
Manifest Destiny, 75
Mao Zedong, 118
Marshall Plan, 95, 114, 127
Marx, Karl, 22, 136
McCarthyism,52, 96, 207
McGann, William, 86
McVeigh, Timothy,157, 159
Mead, Walter R., 45
Mehta, Uday, 42–3, 44, 170
Mexico, 48, 49, 60, 85, 133, 137, 202
Middle East, 4, 18, 66, 68, 76, 112,
        114–115, 131, 155, 182–191,
        204
    McJihad coalition in, 186–191
    US initiative on (2003), 181
    US loss of power in, 185–186,
        188–189
migration, 140
Miller, Geoffrey, 166
Mitchell, Tim,186–187
Mobil 6
Molotov, Vyacheslav, 102
Monroe Doctrine, viii, 18, 48, 49–50,
        57, 59, 60, 64, 65, 67, 77, 99,
        103, 107
    global, viii, 73–74, 75, 77, 84,
        125–126, 147, 181, 207
Morgan, House of, 91
Morgenthau, Henry, 92, 93

N

NAFTA, 202
Nagasaki, 113
nationalism, American, 15–16, 18,
        30–36, 77, 81, 116, 201,
        202–204
    and hardening of borders,
        201–204
    Arab, 185, 186
    contradiction with globalism, 16,
        26, 77, 78, 125, 200–204
    and internationalism, 35–36
native Americans, 46–7, 168
Negri, Antonio, 51
neoconservatism, vii, 16–21, 25, 29,
        40, 41, 52, 58, 153, 174, 194,
        204, 205, 208–209
neoliberalism, vii, 16–21, 29, 34,
        40–42, 52, 58, 133, 135,
        142–146, 194, 201, 208–210
New Deal, 90
New Guinea, 66
New York City, 131
Newfoundland, 92
Nicaragua, 196
Nike Corp., 138–139, 180
Nixon, Richard, 129, 133
Norway, 196

O

oil, 6–7, 24, 114–115, 131, 132
    peak, 183
    war for, 182
O'Neill, Paul, 21, 122, 148, 155
OPEC, 131, 133
Open Door policy, 72, 92, 94, 95, 179
Orwell, George, 109–110
Ottoman Empire, 3, 4, 66, 75

P

Pacific, 66
Paine, Tom 32, 63

Pakistan, 118
Palestine, 4, 6, 12, 112, 114, 115, 158, 175, 186
Palmer raids, 79
Pan African Congress, 68
Panama, 65, 147
Paris Peace Conference (1919), 5, 55–61, 63–75, 87, 89, 102
    territorial issues at, 69
    self determination at, 66–68, 72–73, 74
Patriot Act (2001), 206
Penn, William, 62–63
Pentagon, 151, 163
Perle, Richard, 153
Philippines, 47, 71, 118
Platt Amendment (1904), 167
Poland, 59, 69, 102, 104–105, 115, 203
Popper, Karl, 142
Progressivism, 38, 60
Project for a New American Century (PNAC), 16–20, 58, 152–153
property, private, 85–86
Puerto Rico, 47, 71, 167, 168, 169

R

racism, 9, 28, 32–33, 38, 79, 105–106, 118
Reagan, Ronald, 19, 29, 122, 123, 133, 142, 145, 158, 186
realism,
    new liberal, 170–176
    (*see* also idealism)
Red Cross, 162
Red Scare, 207
Republican Party, vii, 7, 20–21, 57, 60, 64–65, 77, 208
revolution, 64, 79, 82, 120, 160
American, 160, 172
Soviet, 79
Richard, the Lionhearted, 152

Rockefeller, Nelson, 103
rogue states, 10
Roosevelt, Eleanor, 112
Roosevelt, Franklin D., viii, 39, 86–88, 90, 91–2, 96, 98–109, 114, 116–117, 120, 147, 181, 190, 205, 208
"Four Policemen" of, 105
Roosevelt, Teddy, 50, 51, 60, 87
Rostow, Walt, 142
Rousseau, Jean Jacques, 30–32, 63
Royal Dutch Shell, 6
Rubin, Robert, 21
Rumania, 115
Rumsfeld, Donald, 19, 152, 153, 154, 163–164, 197, 205
Russell, Bertrand. 204
Russia, 11, 13, 39, 40–41, 64, 134, 175

S

Saud, Ibn, 115
Saudi Arabia, 5, 115, 156, 183, 186–189, 190
Schmitt, Carl, 173
Schröder, Gerhard., 8, 40, 192
Schumpeter, Joseph, 22,
Seattle, Battle of (1999), 201–202
    general strike (1919), 79
September 11th, vii, ix, 8–10, 150–152, 153, 154, 156, 161, 188, 190, 191, 192, 201, 209
Serbia, 147
Shantung, 66
Sharon, Ariel, 158, 175, 186
Shi'a, 3, 5
Singapore, 132
Smith, Adam, 30–32, 34, 45, 136, 145, 146
socialists, 38–39, 63, 64, 79, 81, 142, 207

Soviet Union, 64, 78, 80, 92, 94, 96,
    97–98, 100–108, 111, 113,
    114, 124, 127, 135, 183, 185,
    187
Spain, 47, 71, 196
Stalin, Joseph, 103– 108, 113–114,
    115, 117
Standard Oil of New Jersey, 6, 183
stars and stripes, 1–2, 10, 16, 26, 30,
    152
State Department, 90, 93–94, 95, 96,
    97–99, 101, 108, 110, 111,
    112
Stettinius, Edward, 102, 103
Strong, George, 109
Sudan, 147
suffrage, 38
Sunni, 3, 5
superimperialism, 25
Sykes-Picot agreement, 4
Syria, 4, 6

T

Taft, Robert A, 177
Taft-Hartley Act (1947), 117
Taiwan, 132
Taliban, the, 161, 196
Tehran, 104, 115
Terror, the, 160
terrorism, 8–9, 157–161
    clash of, 210
    and class, 159–160
    state v. private market, 210
    war on, viii, ix, 152–176, 181, 190,
        191, 198, 204, 207, 210
    war of, 161, 173, 175, 210, 215
Texas, 85–86
Thailand, 114, 132
Thatcher, Margaret, 29, 40, 142
Third World, 114, 127, 132, 137
    industrialization of, 95, 114
Tito, 115
trade, 13–15, 72, 94–95, 116, 144–145

Treasury Department, 21, 91, 93–4,
    95, 97, 110, 128, 144, 200
Truman, Harry, 104, 114–118
    Point IV program of, 114
Turkey, 5–6

U

Ukraine, 103, 107
uneven development, 127–128, 137
United Fruit, 49–50, 120
United Nations, 20, 39, 54, 83–84, 88,
    97–108, 111–113, 119, 127,
    157, 202
    and Iraq, 10, 15,153, 155, 156,
        192, 196
    national basis of, 111–113, 116
    San Francisco founding
        conference of, 90, 102–108
    veto power in, 105, 192
United States, 9–10, 23, 61, 88, 100
    agricultural policy of, 14, 15
    as 'new nation', 30–31
    colonialism of, 47–50, 167, 169
    constitution of, 31, 41, 99
    economic crises in, 91, 128
    economic expansion in, 47–49,
        70–72, 78, 126–131
    financial system of, 92–94,
        128–135, 203
    global ambition of, vii, viii, 2,
        11–16, 17–20, 25–27, 41–2,
        51, 72–74, 75–76, 89, 90, 96,
        107–110, 125–126,
        146–148, 169, 170, 185, 191,
        201–210
    contradictions of, 35–36, 78,
        116, 125, 155, 182, 194,
        201–204
    failures of, xiii–ix, 76–81,
        112–113, 116–120, 169,
        195–204, 205–206, 207–210
    impossibility of, 198–200
    opposition to, 77–81, 117–119

perceived alternatives to, 189–190
imperialism of, 7, 11, 18–19, 22–24, 25–27, 30, 43–44, 46–52, 76, 169, 205, 207–210
isolation of, vii, 15, 78, 86, 195–196, 199
military budget of, 198–199, 200
transition to geo-economic power, 50, 70–72, 74, 76–78, 147, 181–182
unilateralism of, 10, 13, 20, 25, 108, 193–194
US Congress, 11, 62, 65, 77, 94, 154, 163, 167
US Federal Reserve, 128
US Senate, 39, 77–78, 88, 203
USSR (*see* Soviet Union)
US Supreme Court, 47, 168, 169
US Virgin Islands, 49
Uzbekistan, 24

V

Vandenberg, Arthur, 105
Versailles Treaty, 77, 109, 203
Vidal, Gore, 60, 155
Vietnam, 120
    war in, 11, 50, 71, 118, 128, 196, 198, 208
Volcker, Paul, 132, 133, 142

W

Wahhabism, 186–187
Wall Street, 21, 22, 131
Washington Consensus, vii, 144
Washington, George, 160

Washington riot (1919), 80
Weber, Max 160
welfare, corporate, 21
welfare state, 120, 126–127, 145
Welles, Sumner, 103
White, Dexter, 92, 93, 94–5, 96
Williams, William Appleman, 50, 72, 74
Wills, Gary, 60
Wilson, Woodrow, viii, 38, 51, 54–81, 84, 87, 88–89, 90, 91, 96, 104, 105, 120, 147, 152, 181, 190, 205, 207, 208
    and League of Nations, 55, 61–68, 101, 107
    opposition to, 77–81, 203
    and popular repression, 38–39, pragmatic idealism of, 72, 74, 89
Wolfowitz, Paul, 19, 153, 154, 190
World Bank, 29, 41, 83–84, 94, 95, 97, 143, 144
World Trade Center (1993 bombing), 190
World Trade Organization (WTO), 13–15, 83–84, 144, 201
World War I, 4, 27, 56, 61–62, 63, 91, 118, 155
World War II, 27, 39, 84, 85, 86, 89–90, 108, 118, 155
    second front in, 100
W.R. Grace, 49–50
Wright, Steven, 122

Y

Yalta, 104–105, 115
Yugoslavia, 115